everyday
Asian

everyday
Asian

MURDOCH
BOOKS

contents

Stir-fry Ingredients

Stir-frying is a quick, easy and healthy method of cooking, which combines the best of fresh produce and exotic flavours. Most wok-cooked recipes are obviously Asian in origin, and so may require a trip to an Asian supermarket, grocer or local Chinatown. However, ingredients such as bok choy and mirin are becoming popular and are now widely available in local supermarkets.

Annatto seeds

These are small red triangular-shaped seeds with a subtle flavour and vivid colour. Used extensively in Latin American cooking, they were introduced to the Philippines by the Spanish traders. Once they have been fried in oil, the seeds are usually removed and the coloured oil is used in the dish. Annatto seeds are used by the Chinese to give their roast pork its characteristic pinkish red colouring.

Asian shallots

These are small onions with a papery reddish, purple skin, commonly used in Asian cookery. These grow in bulbs like garlic and are sold in segments that look like large cloves of garlic. They have a concentrated flavour and are easy to slice and grind. You can use red onions as a substitute—one small red onion to 4–6 shallots. French shallots are not a good substitute—the flavour is quite different.

Banana leaves

The large pliable green leaves of the banana tree are used throughout Asia as disposable plates and platters, as well as for wrapping food that is to be baked or steamed. Before use, remove the centre stalk, rinse the leaves in cold water and then blanch briefly in boiling water to soften. They are available in packets from Asian food stores if you don't have access to fresh. If they are to be used for wrapping food for cooking, foil can be used instead.

Barbecued duck pancakes

These round wrappers, made with wheat flour, are traditionally eaten as part of the Chinese meal, Peking duck, traditional to the north of the country. Crisp duck skin, raw spring onion and hoisin sauce are wrapped in the pancakes. The pancakes are sold frozen at Asian supermarkets or ask for them when you buy your barbecued duck.

Barbecued Chinese duck

These are ducks that have been spiced and glazed and then spit-roasted over a barbecue. The ducks are available from Chinese barbecue shops, which can be found in any Chinatown. You can ask the vendor to chop, shred or bone the duck for you if the recipe requires it. If you can't find barbecued duck, you could use home-roasted duck, but the flavour will not be as good (and the dish not as convenient).

Barbecued Chinese pork (*char siew*)

This is pork that has been marinated in five-spice powder, soy sauce, sugar and annatto and then spit-roasted over a barbecue. It has a strong flavour and particularly distinctive reddish-pink flesh, coloured by the annatto seeds in the marinade. The pork is available from Chinese barbecue shops, which can be found in any Chinatown. If you can't find barbecued pork, you could use home-roasted pork, but the flavour will not be as good (and the dish not as convenient).

Basil

Thai basil has a strong aroma and flavour, so don't use more than is stated in the recipe. There are three varieties most commonly used. *Bai horapha* tastes rather like anise, looks like sweet basil and is used in Thai curry dishes. *Bai manglaek* has a lemony flavour, tiny leaves and is usually sprinkled over salads. *Bai grapao* has a clove-like taste and purple-reddish tinged leaves. It doesn't store well, so buy it at the last minute. European basil can be used as a substitute for all varieties if necessary. Thai basil is often called 'holy basil' because it is grown around temples.

Bean sprouts

Used mainly in salads and as a stir-fry vegetable, soy bean sprouts are crunchy, white short sprouts. Discard any that are limp or brown. They are highly perishable so keep in the fridge and use within three days of purchase. Traditionally, the scraggly ends are removed before use.

Black beans

Salted black beans are available canned or in vacuum packs from Asian stores. They should be whole and dark and must be rinsed in cold water to get rid of their excess saltiness. Chop the beans before cooking for a more robust flavour. There are two different types of black beans—the Chinese version (which we use in this book) and the Mexican version. The Mexican ones are also known as 'turtle' beans and are often used for thick Caribbean soups.

Black fungus

This is a Chinese ingredient that is also used in some Thai dishes. It has no real flavour but is used for its chewy texture. It looks like dried black wrinkled paper but, after soaking in water for about 10 minutes, it swells and resembles wavy seaweed or jelly. Stored in its dried form it will keep indefinitely. It is also known as 'wood ear' or 'cloud ear' mushroom.

Bok choy

This popular Chinese vegetable (also known as Chinese cabbage or pak choi) has fleshy white stems and dark green leaves. The whole leaf can be chopped and used for stir-frying, once the tough ends have been cut off. Baby bok choy is smaller and more tender. Shanghai bok choy has pale green stems.

Candlenuts

These large cream nuts, similar to macadamias in shape but with a drier texture, cannot be eaten raw as their oil is thought to be toxic. They are ground and used to thicken sauces and curries, and in Indonesia and Malaysia they are used to make candles, which is how they came by their name.

Chillies

Chillies make up one branch of the capsicum family (the other branch being sweet peppers). Red chillies are simply ripened green chillies, which means they are a little sweeter (just like red and green capsicums). Names of chillies vary from country to country, with growers making up new names all the time. For that reason, most recipes will simply state 1 red chilli or 1 green chilli. Dried chillies and chilli powder are also available.

Bird's eye chillies are the smallest and hottest variety of all. From 1–3 cm (^{1}/$_2$–1 ^{1}/$_4$ inches) long, they are available fresh, dried or pickled in brine.

Small red chillies, approximately 5 cm (2 inches) long are the chillies used to make chilli powder and chilli flakes. They are those most commonly used in Thai cooking.

Medium chillies, 10–15 cm (4–6 inches) long, are most commonly used in Indonesian and Malaysian cooking. They are thin chillies and are hot but not overpowering, with the seeds the hottest part.

Large red and green chillies, 15–20 cm (6–8 inches) long, these thick chillies are used in Northern Thai cooking. The ripe red chillies are fiery. To avoid skin irritation, take great care when chopping or seeding chillies. Wear rubber gloves if you can, otherwise, wash your hands thoroughly in warm soapy water after chopping and before touching your face or eyes. If you like a hot curry, leave the chilli seeds in. In you prefer a milder flavour, discard the fiery seeds and membrane. Whole chillies freeze well in plastic bags and can be chopped while frozen. Some chillies are available dried and are soaked in water to soften before use.

Chinese broccoli

Chinese broccoli (*gai larn*) or Chinese kale has smooth round stems with dark green leaves and small white flowers. The stems are the part most commonly eaten.

Chinese dried mushrooms

These impart a distinct flavour to the dish and are used in Asian recipes with a Chinese influence. Store in an airtight container in a cool place and soak before use.

Choy sum

This flowering Chinese cabbage has green stems and yellow flowers. It is often confused with *gai larn* (Chinese broccoli), which is similar in appearance but has white flowers instead of yellow. The two are interchangeable in recipes.

Coriander

Also known, in its fresh form, as cilantro, coriander is the most commonly used herb in Thai cooking. The whole plant can be used—the root, stem, seeds and leaves. The seeds are roasted and then ground in a spice mill and used in curry pastes. Fresh coriander is available from greengrocers, supermarkets and Asian food stores, or in pots from nurseries.

The leaves (which look very similar to those of continental parsley) are used for their fresh, peppery flavour and as a garnish. For storage, wash and dry the fresh herbs before placing them in plastic bags in the fridge, where they will keep for 5–6 days. Dried coriander is not a suitable substitute for fresh.

Crisp-fried onion and garlic

Finely sliced garlic cloves or onions are deep-fried until crisp. They are often added to stir-fries just before serving, as a garnish. If you don't have time to make your own, you can buy them in packets. To make your own, finely slice an onion and garlic and cook over low heat in oil, stirring until crisp and golden. Drain well on paper towels and then season liberally with salt. Serve immediately so they are crisp.

Dashi

This is the basic stock of Japanese cuisine. Made with dried kelp and dried bonito (a fish), it is available packaged in ground form, as granules or in flakes—add hot water to make up to stock.

Dried lily buds

These Chinese specialities are used for their texture and subtle flavour. They have no real substitute, but could be omitted without radically altering the flavour of the dish.

Dried mandarin peel

More commonly used as a seasoning in Chinese slow-cooked dishes, you will also find these adding flavour to a couple of stir-fry dishes. Dried mandarin and tangerine peel are easily prepared at home and can be stored in an airtight container for months. Use a vegetable peeler to slice the peel thinly. Cut the strips into small pieces and carefully scrape off any remaining pith or flesh. Place the pieces in a single layer on a baking tray and dry in a preheated 180°C (350°F/Gas 4) oven for 15 minutes. Three mandarins will produce about a third of a cup of dried peel.

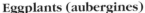

Dried shrimp

Tiny salted shrimp that have been dried in the sun, these are added to stir-fries for their strong flavour.

Eggplants (aubergines)

There are many different sizes, shapes and colours of eggplant now available. Tiny pea-sized eggplants are available in some Asian food stores and are excellent for stir-fries, although they can sometimes be a little bitter. Small long lady-finger eggplants are also used. Large European eggplants can be used, but should be cut up small for quick and even stir-frying.

Fish sauce

This brown, salty sauce with its characteristically strong fishy aroma is an important ingredient in Thai and Vietnamese cookery. It is made from small fish that have been fermented in the sun for a long time and is usually added as a seasoning at the end of cooking to balance sweetness and add saltiness. The smell from the sauce can be so off-putting that people using it for the first time may think there is something wrong with it.

Galangal

Related to ginger and quite similar looking, galangal is pinkish in colour and has a distinct peppery flavour. Use fresh galangal where possible and be careful when handling that you don't get the juice on your clothes or hands, as it stains. Dried galangal must be soaked in hot water before use. Galangal powder is also available.

Ginger

This delicious aromatic ingredient is important in Asian cooking. Fresh ginger is now readily available—buy firm, unwrinkled rhizomes and store them in a plastic bag so they don't dry out. To prepare ginger for cooking, simply remove the skin with a vegetable peeler and then either grate, finely slice or shred the ginger before stir-frying. Very young ginger may not even require peeling.

Green pawpaw

These are not a different variety, but merely underripe pawpaws. To shred the green pawpaw, peel it and slice it finely. It is sometimes blanched lightly before shredding.

Hoisin sauce

This thick reddish brown sauce, made from soy beans, sugar, spices and red rice, has a sweet spicy flavour and is popular for stir-fries. It is also used as a dipping sauce or for glazes. Available from Asian food stores and supermarkets.

Hot bean paste

Made from fermented soy beans and chilli, this sauce can be very hot and should be added very lightly.

Kaffir limes and leaves

A knobbly dark-skinned lime with a very strong lime fragrance and flavour. The leaves are finely shredded for use in stir-fries. The rind is also very pungent and is often grated for adding to dishes. The leaves are available in packets from Asian grocers.

Kecap manis

This is a thick sweet soy sauce that is widely used in Indonesian and Malaysian cooking as a seasoning or sauce. If it's not available, use soy sauce sweetened with a little soft brown sugar.

Lemon grass

This aromatic fresh herb is used in curry pastes and stir-fries, as well as myriad other Asian dishes. The stems can be up to 60 cm (2 feet) long. Trim the base, remove the tough outer layers and finely slice, chop or pound the white inner layers in a mortar and pestle or processor. For pastes, use the tender white portion just above the root. The whole stem, trimmed and washed thoroughly, can be added to dishes that are to be simmered, and then removed before serving. Dried lemon grass is available and needs soaking for half an hour before use. The flavour of fresh is superior.

Mirin

This low-alcohol rice wine, made from sake, is used in Japanese dishes. The sugar content helps to glaze food when it is cooked. Choose pure mirin as some brands are a sweet seasoning type that have corn syrup and salt added. If mirin is not available, you can use dry sherry or sweet white wine.

Miso

This thick fermented paste is made from soy beans and other ingredients, including wheat and rice. It is available in many varieties, including light brown, red, brown, yellow and white, each differing in flavour and texture.

Mushrooms

Shiitake, oyster and enoki are all types of mushroom used in Asian cookery and are all usually available fresh from supermarkets. Shiitake mushrooms, originally from Japan and Korea, have a distinctive meaty flavour. These large, dark mushrooms are now cultivated worldwide and are often found in the USA under the name *golden oak*. Often sold dried as 'winter' or 'Chinese black dried' mushrooms. Oyster mushrooms are delicately flavoured and take their name because they have a slight taste of oysters. Enoki mushrooms are also known as enokitake mushrooms. They come in clumps of long thin stems with tiny white caps and have to be gently separated before use. Available fresh and dried. Straw mushrooms, grown in straw, have globe-shaped caps and no stems. They are available in cans and have a musty flavour.

Oyster sauce

This is a Cantonese staple, found in many Thai dishes that have a Chinese influence. It is made from dried oysters and is a rich salty sauce, used for flavouring. Refrigerate after opening to prevent mould forming.

Palm sugar

This caramel-flavoured sugar is obtained from either the palmyra palm or sugar palm and is bought either in block form or in jars. The colour ranges from pale golden to very dark brown. Palm sugar is thick and crumbly and can be gently melted or grated before adding to dishes. Soft brown sugar is an adequate replacement if necessary.

Rice vinegar and seasoned rice vinegar

Rice vinegar is a mild, sweet, delicately flavoured vinegar made from rice. Seasoned rice vinegar is similar, but has sugar and salt added to it.

Seasoning sauce

This thin salty soy bean seasoning sauce is used in Asian cooking to enhance the flavour of dishes. It is also sold under the name Golden Mountain sauce.

Sesame oil

This very aromatic oil, made from roasted sesame seeds, is used in Thai recipes that have a Chinese influence. Use it sparingly, as it has quite a strong rich flavour and a little goes a long way. Rather than using it for stir-frying, you will often find a teaspoonful of it added to the cooking oil to add flavour.

Sesame and seaweed sprinkle

Seaweed is really only popular in Japan, where it is eaten as a vegetable. Wakame is the most famous variety, then kombu and nori. This combination of dried and finely chopped nori, roasted sesame seeds and salt is used as a seasoning to be sprinkled on noodle dishes after cooking.

Shoshoyu (Japanese soy sauce)

Also known as shoyu. This is much lighter and sweeter than Chinese soy sauce and not thick like kecap manis. It is naturally brewed from soya beans and grains such as wheat or barley, and so needs to be refrigerated after opening.

Shrimp paste *(bagoong)*

This is a paste made from shrimps or prawns that have been salted and fermented in earthenware pots. It is used as a condiment as well as an ingredient in stir-fries.

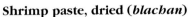

Shrimp paste, dried *(blachan)*

Made from prawns or shrimps that have been dried, salted and pounded into blocks, this has a pungent smell and, once opened, should be sealed in an airtight container in the fridge (the paste itself does not require refrigeration, but this will reduce the aroma). It should always be roasted (usually wrapped up in a foil parcel) or fried before adding to a recipe. Also known as *belacci*, *terasi* or *kapi*.

Sichuan pepper

Sichuan (Szechwan) pepper is a tiny red berry not related to ordinary peppercorns. It is aromatic and is one of the ingredients in five spice powder. Remove the black seeds and dry-fry it to bring out its full flavour before using it in cooking.

Snake beans

These are long, deep green, stringless beans that grow up to 30 cm (12 inches) long. They are cut into short lengths for stir-frying. They do not have a very strong flavour and are easy to prepare.

Soy sauce

This popular dark salty sauce of Chinese origin is made from fermented roasted soy beans, another grain (usually wheat) and brine. It is aged for up to two years before being filtered and bottled. Soy sauce is indispensable in Asian cooking and is now widely available. It should be kept in the fridge after opening.

Star anise

This dark brown star-shaped pod with its distinctive aniseed flavour is used whole to flavour curries, or ground in pastes.

Tamari

This dark, richly flavoured Japanese soy sauce is made from rice rather than wheat. It can be used as a seasoning or dipping sauce.

Tamarind

Tamarind is available in a variety of forms and this fibrous pod is used to give an acidic flavour to dishes. Most commonly found as a concentrate—a sour liquid made from the fruits of the tamarind tree. It is also available as a pulp, which must be soaked in hot water for 5 minutes, then strained before use.

Tempeh

Similar to tofu, tempeh is made from fermented soy beans. Quite firm in texture, it is suitable for most types of cooking. It is popular with vegetarians and vegans as, like tofu, when it is marinated it successfully takes on the flavour of the marinade.

Tofu (bean curd)

Silken tofu: A very soft tofu often used in soups. Take care when cooking with it or it will break up, so not usually used for stir-fries.

Silken firm tofu: Slightly firmer than silken tofu, it holds its shape a little better. More often used in soups than stir-fries.

Firm tofu: This soft tofu will hold its shape when cooking and soak up marinade flavours. Suitable for stir-frying.

Hard tofu: Rubbery and firm, this won't break up during cooking. Use for stir-frying.

Tofu tempeh: Tofu and tempeh are combined and pressed together. Use in the same way as firm tofu.

Deep-fried tofu puffs: Tofu is aerated and then deep-fried. This variety is excellent for stir-fries.

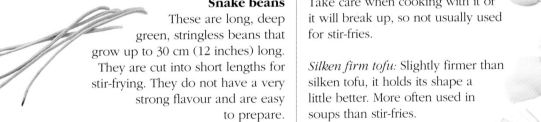

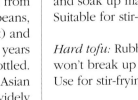

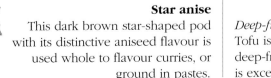

soups & snacks

SAN CHOY BAU

Preparation time: 25 minutes
  + 10 minutes soaking
Total cooking time: 10 minutes
Serves 4

4 dried Chinese mushrooms
oil, for cooking
1/4 cup (30 g/1 oz) slivered almonds,
    chopped
125 g (4 oz) water chestnuts, drained
    and finely chopped
1 carrot, finely chopped
4 spring onions, finely chopped
250 g (8 oz) lean pork mince
4 coriander roots, finely chopped
1 tablespoon grated fresh ginger
12 lettuce leaves
hoisin sauce, to serve

SAUCE
1 tablespoon light soy sauce
1 tablespoon lime juice
1 teaspoon sesame oil
1/4 cup (15 g/1/2 oz) chopped fresh
    coriander
2 tablespoons chopped fresh mint

1 Soak the mushrooms in a small bowl of hot water for 10 minutes, or until softened. Discard the tough stems and finely chop the mushroom caps.
2 To make the sauce, combine the light soy sauce, lime juice, oil, coriander and mint in a small jug.
3 Heat the wok until very hot, add 1 tablespoon of the oil and swirl it around to coat the side. Add the almonds, water chestnuts, carrot and spring onion to the wok and stir-fry for 1 minute, or until they are lightly cooked but not browned—they should still be crisp. Remove from the wok and set aside.

4 Reheat the wok and add 1 tablespoon of the oil. Stir-fry the pork mince, coriander root, ginger and mushrooms over medium–high heat for 2–3 minutes, or until the pork changes colour, but do not overcook the pork or it will be tough.
5 Add the sauce and stir to combine. Return the vegetable mixture to the wok and stir-fry for 1–2 minutes, or until heated through and the mixture is well combined. Spoon the pork mixture into the lettuce leaves and sprinkle with the hoisin sauce, to taste. Serve more hoisin sauce for dipping.

NUTRITION PER SERVE
Protein 3.5 g; Fat 20 g; Carbohydrate 15 g; Dietary Fibre 5 g; Cholesterol 0 mg; 1525 kJ (365 Cal)

Water chestnuts are available canned. Drain them and then chop.

Soak the Chinese mushrooms, then discard the tough stems and finely chop them.

Stir-fry the pork mince with the coriander root, ginger and mushrooms.

THAI FISH CAKES

Preparation time: 20 minutes
Total cooking time: 20 minutes
Serves 4–6

500 g (1 lb) redfish fillets, chopped
1 stem lemon grass, white part
    only, chopped
2 tablespoons fish sauce
5 spring onions, chopped
3 tablespoons chopped fresh
    coriander
1 clove garlic, crushed
140 ml (4¹/₂ fl oz) can coconut milk
1 tablespoon sweet chilli sauce
1 egg
5 snake beans, finely sliced
oil, for shallow-frying
200 g (6¹/₂ oz) mixed lettuce leaves

SAUCE
¹/₃ cup (90 g/3 oz) sugar
2 tablespoons sweet chilli sauce
¹/₂ small Lebanese cucumber, diced

1 Place the fish, lemon grass, fish sauce, spring onion, coriander, garlic, coconut milk, sweet chilli sauce and egg in a food processor or blender and blend until smooth. Transfer to a bowl and fold in the snake beans. With wet hands, shape into twelve 7 cm (2³/₄ inch) fish cakes, about 1 cm (¹/₂ inch) high. Place on a plate, cover and refrigerate until ready to use.
2 For the sauce, stir the sugar and ¹/₃ cup (80 ml/2³/₄ fl oz) water in a small saucepan over low heat for 2 minutes, or until all the sugar has dissolved. Increase the heat and simmer for 5 minutes, or until slightly thickened. Remove from the heat and stir in the sweet chilli sauce. Cool and stir in the diced cucumber.

3 Heat the oil in a deep, heavy-based frying pan and cook the fish cakes over medium heat for 1–2 minutes on each side, or until cooked through.
4 Divide the lettuce among the plates and arrange the fish cakes on top. Serve with the sauce.

NUTRITION PER SERVE (6)
Protein 21 g; Fat 11 g; Carbohydrate 19 g; Dietary Fibre 1.5 g; Cholesterol 88.5 mg; 1055 kJ (250 Cal)

Shape the mixture into 12 patties about 7 cm (2³/₄ inch) across and 1 cm (¹/₂ inch) high.

Remove from the heat and stir the sweet chilli sauce into the sugar syrup.

Cook the fish cakes on both sides, turning with a spatula, until cooked through.

CHICKEN CURRY PUFFS

Preparation time: 1 hour 30 minutes +
    30 minutes chilling
Total cooking time: 35–45 minutes
Makes about 36

2 tablespoons oil
400 g (13 oz) chicken mince
2 cloves garlic, crushed
1 onion, finely chopped
3 coriander roots, finely chopped
2 teaspoons ground turmeric
1½ teaspoons ground cumin
3 teaspoons ground coriander
1 small potato, peeled and very
    finely diced
1 tablespoon chopped fresh coriander
    leaves and stems
3 teaspoons soft brown sugar
½ teaspoon ground black pepper
2 small red chillies, finely chopped
¼ cup (60 ml/2 fl oz) fish sauce
1 tablespoon lime juice
oil, extra, for deep-frying
chilli sauce or satay sauce, to serve

PASTRY
1½ cups (185 g/6 oz) plain flour
½ cup (90 g/3 oz) rice flour
½ teaspoon salt
60 g (2 oz) butter
½ cup (125 ml/4 fl oz) coconut milk

1 Heat the oil in a wok or frying pan.
Add the mince and cook over high
heat for 3 minutes, or until it is starting
to brown. Break up any lumps of
mince with a fork as it cooks. Add the
crushed garlic, onion, coriander roots,
ground turmeric, cumin and coriander,
and the potato to the wok. Stir-fry over
medium heat for about 5 minutes, or
until the mince and potato are tender.

2 Add the fresh coriander, sugar,
pepper, chilli, fish sauce and lime juice.
Stir until well combined and most of
the liquid has evaporated, then remove
from the heat and allow to cool.
3 To make the pastry, sift the flours
and salt into a medium bowl and rub
in the butter until the mixture is fine
and crumbly. Make a well in the
centre, add the coconut milk and mix
with a knife until the mixture forms
a dough. Gently knead until the dough
is smooth. Cover with plastic wrap and
refrigerate for 30 minutes.
4 Divide the dough in half. Roll out
one half on a lightly floured surface
until it is about 3 mm (⅛ inch) thick
and then cut into circles with an 8 cm
(3 inch) cutter.
5 Place 2 teaspoons of the filling
in the centre of each circle, brush the
edges of the pastry lightly with water
and fold over to enclose the filling;
press the edges to seal. Repeat with
the remaining half of the dough,
re-rolling the scraps until the dough
and the filling are all used.
6 Heat the oil in a large wok or pan.
Do not put too much oil in the wok—
it should be only half full. Deep-fry
the puffs, in batches, until puffed and
browned. Remove from oil with a wire
mesh drainer, slotted spoon or tongs
and drain on paper towels. Serve hot
with chilli sauce or satay sauce.

NUTRITION PER PUFF
Protein 3.5 g; Fat 8 g; Carbohydrate 7 g; Dietary
Fibre 0.5 g; Cholesterol 15 mg; 463 kJ (111 Cal)

HINT: If time is short, use about eight
sheets of ready-rolled puff pastry
instead of making the pastry.

Use a spoon or fork to break up any lumps of
mince as it cooks.

Stir the ingredients in the wok until well combined
and the liquid has evaporated.

Add the coconut milk and mix with a knife until the
mixture forms a dough.

Cut the rolled out dough into circles, using an 8 cm (3 inch) cutter.

Fold the pastry over to enclose the filling and then press the edges to seal.

Add the curry puffs to the hot oil, cooking only a few at a time.

TOM YUM GOONG

Preparation time: 25 minutes
Total cooking time: 45 minutes
Serves 4–6

500 g (1 lb) raw medium prawns
1 tablespoon oil
2 tablespoons tom yum paste
2 tablespoons tamarind purée
2 teaspoons ground turmeric
1 teaspoon chopped small red
    chillies
4 kaffir lime leaves, shredded
2 tablespoons fish sauce
2 tablespoons lime juice

2 teaspoons grated palm sugar
    or soft brown sugar
kaffir lime leaves, shredded, extra,
    to garnish

1 Peel the prawns, leaving the tails intact. Remove the vein from each prawn. Reserve the shells and heads. Cover and refrigerate the prawn meat. Heat the oil in a wok and cook the shells and heads over medium heat, stirring frequently, for 10 minutes, or until the shells turn orange.
2 Add 1 cup (250 ml/8 fl oz) water and the tom yum paste to the wok. Bring to the boil and cook for 5 minutes, or until reduced slightly.

Add another 2 litres water, bring to the boil, reduce the heat and simmer for 20 minutes. Strain, discard the shells and heads, and return the stock to the pan.
3 Add the tamarind, turmeric, chilli and lime leaves to the pan, bring to the boil and cook for 2 minutes. Add the prawns and cook for 5 minutes, or until pink. Stir in the fish sauce, lime juice and sugar. Garnish with shredded kaffir lime leaves.

NUTRITION PER SERVE (6)
Protein 15 g; Fat 5 g; Carbohydrate 11 g;
Dietary Fibre 1.3 g; Cholesterol 158 mg;
608 kJ (145 Cal)

Finely shred the kaffir lime leaves with a sharp knife.

Cook the water and tom yum paste until reduced slightly.

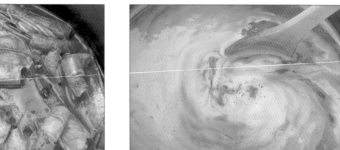

Stir in the tamarind, turmeric, chilli and lime leaves and cook for 2 minutes.

WON TON STACKS WITH TUNA AND GINGER

Preparation time: 20 minutes
Total cooking time: 10 minutes
Makes 24

1½ tablespoons sesame seeds
12 fresh won ton wrappers
½ cup (125 ml/4 fl oz) peanut or
     vegetable oil
150 g (5 oz) piece fresh tuna fillet
     (see NOTE)
¼ cup (60 g/2 oz) Japanese
     mayonnaise
50 g (1¾ oz) pickled ginger
50 g (1¾ oz) snow pea sprouts
2 teaspoons mirin
2 teaspoons soy sauce
¼ teaspoon sugar

1 Lightly toast the sesame seeds in a small dry frying pan over low heat for 2–3 minutes, or until golden.
2 Cut the won ton wrappers into quarters to give 48 squares in total. Heat the oil in a small saucepan over medium heat and cook the wrappers in batches for 1–2 minutes, or until they are golden and crisp. Drain on crumpled paper towels.
3 Thinly slice the tuna into 24 slices. Spoon approximately ¼ teaspoon of the mayonnaise onto 24 of the won ton squares. Place a slice of tuna on the mayonnaise and top with a little of the pickled ginger, snow pea sprouts and sesame seeds.
4 Mix the mirin, soy sauce and sugar together in a small bowl and drizzle a little over each stack. Season with pepper. Top with the remaining

24 won ton squares (lids). Serve immediately or the stacks will absorb the dressing and become soggy.

NUTRITION PER STACK
Protein 2.5 g; Fat 6 g; Carbohydrate 4 g; Dietary Fibre 0.5 g; Cholesterol 3.5 mg; 335 kJ (80 Cal)

NOTE: For this recipe, you need good-quality tuna. Sashimi tuna is the best quality, but if you can't get that, buy only the freshest tuna with as little sinew as possible.

THINK AHEAD: The won ton wrappers can be fried the day before serving. Store them in an airtight container large enough that they are not cramped. Place sheets of paper towels between each layer.

Using a sharp knife, cut the won ton wrappers into four equal squares.

Cook the won ton squares in the hot oil until they are crisp and golden.

Using a sharp knife, cut the tuna into very thin, even slices.

PEKING DUCK ROLLS

Preparation time: 35 minutes +
  10 minutes resting
Total cooking time: 5 minutes
Makes 24

1 cup (125 g/4 oz) plain flour
1/2 teaspoon sesame oil
1/2 large Chinese roast duck
6 spring onions, cut into 24 pieces
  6 cm (2 1/2 inches) long
1 Lebanese cucumber, seeded and
  cut into 6 cm x 5 mm (2 1/2 inch x
  1/4 inch) batons
2–3 tablespoons hoisin sauce
2 teaspoons toasted sesame seeds
24 chives, blanched

1 Sift the flour into a small bowl, make a well in the centre, and pour in the sesame oil and 1/2 cup (125 ml/4 fl oz) boiling water. Combine well until the mixture becomes a slightly sticky soft dough. If needed, add a few teaspoons more of boiling water at a time if the mixture is still a bit dry. Knead the dough on a floured work surface for about 5 minutes, or until smooth. Cover and rest for about 10 minutes.
2 Shred the duck meat with your fingers and cut the skin into strips.
3 Roll the dough into a sausage shape and divide into 24 pieces, then roll each piece to an 8–9 cm (3–3 1/2 inch) round with a rolling pin on a lightly floured board. Once they are rolled out, lay them out in a single layer and cover with plastic wrap or a tea towel while you are rolling out the others to prevent them from drying out.
4 Heat a non-stick frying pan over medium–high heat, and dry-fry them in batches for about 20 seconds each side. Do not overcook, or they will be too crispy for rolling. The pancakes should have slight brown speckles on them. Stack each pancake on a plate, and keep warm. If they cool down too much, reheat them by placing on a plate, covering with plastic wrap and microwaving for 20–30 seconds on High, or wrapping them in foil and baking in a warm (170°C/325°F/Gas 3) oven until warmed through.
5 Arrange a piece of spring onion, some cucumber strips, duck flesh and

skin on each pancake. Drizzle with 1/2 teaspoon hoisin sauce and sprinkle with toasted sesame seeds. Roll the pancake up firmly and tie with a blanched chive strip to hold it in place. Serve immediately.

NUTRITION PER ROLL
Protein 4 g; Fat 5 g; Carbohydrate 6 g; Dietary Fibre 0.5 g; Cholesterol 20 mg; 330 kJ (80 Cal)

THINK AHEAD: You can make the pancakes 2–3 days ahead of time and wrap them tightly in plastic wrap until ready to serve. To reheat, put them on a plate, cover with plastic wrap and microwave for 20–30 seconds on high, or wrap them in foil and place in a warm (170°C/ 325°F/Gas 3) oven until warmed through.

Roll each portion of dough into a neat round with a rolling pin.

Tightly roll the pancakes to enclose the filling, then secure with a blanched chive.

STUFFED CHICKEN WINGS

Preparation time: 40 minutes
Total cooking time: 20 minutes
Makes 6

6 large chicken wings

FILLING
3 tablespoons chopped water
   chestnuts
1/2 teaspoon finely chopped garlic
1 tablespoon finely chopped fresh
   coriander leaves
1 1/2 tablespoons fish sauce
1/2 teaspoon ground black pepper
1 spring onion, finely chopped
250 g (8 oz) minced pork

1 Pat the chicken dry with paper towels. To bone the chicken wings, use a small, sharp knife. Starting at the drumstick end, slip the knife down the side of the bone, all the way to the joint, taking care not to pierce the skin. Snap the bone free. Start on the next joint with the point of the knife, taking care not to pierce the elbow.
2 Once the first part of these two bones has been freed, the bones can be pulled out and cut at the knuckle to release. Reshape the wings.
3 To make the filling, combine the water chestnuts, garlic, coriander leaves, fish sauce, pepper, spring onion and pork, mixing thoroughly. Using a teaspoon, stuff the wings evenly with the filling, taking care not to overfill or they will burst during cooking.
4 Place the chicken wings on a lightly oiled steamer, cover and steam over briskly boiling water for 10 minutes. Transfer the wings to a cold, lightly oiled grill tray. Cook the chicken wings under medium heat for 5 minutes on each side or until brown and cooked through.

NUTRITION PER CHICKEN WING
Protein 30 g; Fat 2.5 g; Carbohydrate 1.5 g;
Dietary Fibre 0.5 g; Cholesterol 62 mg;
610 kJ (145 cal)

Slip the knife down the side of the bone, taking care not to pierce the skin.

Pull the bones out and cut at the knuckle to release, then reshape the wings.

Combine the filling ingredients in a large bowl and mix thoroughly.

Place the chicken wings on a lightly oiled steamer and cover with a lid.

CHINESE MUSHROOM AND CHICKEN SOUP

Preparation time: 20 minutes +
10 minutes soaking
Total cooking time: 10 minutes
Serves 4

3 dried Chinese mushrooms
185 g (6 oz) thin dried egg noodles
1 tablespoon oil
4 spring onions, julienned
1 tablespoon soy sauce
2 tablespoons rice wine, mirin
or sherry (see NOTE)
1.25 litres chicken stock
1/2 small barbecued chicken,
shredded

50 g (1³/₄ oz) sliced ham, cut into
strips
1 cup (90 g/3 oz) bean sprouts
fresh coriander leaves, to serve
thinly sliced red chilli, to serve

1 Soak the mushrooms in boiling water for 10 minutes to soften them. Squeeze dry then remove the tough stem from the mushrooms and slice them thinly.

2 Cook the noodles in a large pan of boiling water for 3 minutes, or according to the manufacturer's directions. Drain and cut the noodles into shorter lengths with scissors.

3 Heat the oil in a large heavy-based pan. Add the mushrooms and spring onion. Cook for 1 minute, then add the soy sauce, rice wine and stock. Bring slowly to the boil and cook for 1 minute. Reduce the heat then add the noodles, shredded chicken, ham and bean sprouts. Heat through for 2 minutes without allowing the soup to boil.

4 Use tongs to divide the noodles among four serving bowls, ladle in the remaining mixture, and garnish with coriander leaves and sliced chilli.

NUTRITION PER SERVE
Protein 25 g; Fat 10 g; Carbohydrate 35 g;
Dietary Fibre 3 g; Cholesterol 80 mg;
1426 kJ (340 Cal)

NOTE: Rice wine and mirin are available at Asian food stores.

Use a fork to shred the meat from the barbecued chicken.

Put the mushrooms in a bowl, cover with boiling water and leave to soak.

Cut the noodles into shorter lengths to make them easier to eat.

PRAWN TOASTS

Preparation time: 20 minutes
Total cooking time: 15 minutes
Makes 36

DIPPING SAUCE
1/2 cup (125 ml/4 fl oz) tomato sauce
2 cloves garlic, crushed
2 small fresh red chillies, seeded
    and finely chopped
2 tablespoons hoisin sauce
2 teaspoons Worcestershire sauce

350 g (11 oz) raw medium prawns
1 clove garlic
75 g (2 1/2 oz) canned water chestnuts,
    drained
1 tablespoon chopped fresh coriander
2 cm x 2 cm (3/4 inch x 3/4 inch) piece
    fresh ginger, roughly chopped
2 eggs, separated
1/4 teaspoon white pepper
12 slices white bread, crusts removed
1 cup (155 g/5 oz) sesame seeds
oil, for deep-frying

1 To make the dipping sauce, combine all the ingredients in a small bowl.
2 Peel the prawns and gently pull out the dark vein from each prawn back, starting at the head end. Put the prawns in a food processor with the garlic, water chestnuts, coriander, ginger, egg whites, pepper and 1/4 teaspoon salt, and process for 20–30 seconds, or until smooth.
3 Brush the top of each slice of bread with lightly beaten egg yolk, then spread evenly with the prawn mixture. Sprinkle generously with sesame seeds. Cut each slice of bread into three even strips.
4 Fill a large heavy-based saucepan or deep-fryer one-third full of oil and heat to 180°C (350°F), or until a cube of bread dropped into the oil browns in 15 seconds. Deep-fry the toasts in small batches for 10–15 seconds, or until golden and crisp. Start with the prawn mixture facing down, then turn halfway through. Remove the toasts from the oil with tongs or a slotted spoon and drain on crumpled paper towels. Serve with the dipping sauce.

NUTRITION PER PRAWN TOAST
Protein 3 g; Fat 6.5 g; Carbohydrate 5.5 g; Dietary Fibre 1 g; Cholesterol 19 mg; 383 kJ (92 Cal)

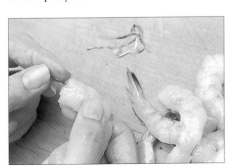

Pull the dark vein out of the prawns from the head end.

Use a food processor to blend the prawn mixture until it is smooth.

Brush the bread with egg yolk, then spread with the prawn mixture.

THAI BEEF SOUP

Preparation time: 20 minutes
Total cooking time: 30 minutes
Serves 4

3 tablespoons oil
1 onion, finely chopped
1 teaspoon grated fresh ginger
1 teaspoon grated galangal
2 cloves garlic, crushed
2 stalks lemongrass (white part only),
   finely chopped
4 red chillies, seeds removed, finely
   chopped
4 macadamia nuts, crushed
1 tablespoon tom yum paste
2 400 g (13 oz) cans coconut milk
3 cups (750 ml/24 fl oz) beef stock
3 teaspoons sugar
100 g (3½ oz) green beans, halved
1 carrot, julienned
300 g (10 oz) fresh Hokkien noodles
100 g (3½ oz) bean sprouts
55 g (2 oz) thinly sliced cooked beef,
   cut into strips
fresh coriander leaves, to garnish

1 Heat the oil in a heavy-based
saucepan, then add the onion, ginger,
galangal, garlic, lemongrass, chilli
and macadamias. Cook, stirring, over
moderate heat for 3–4 minutes, or
until the mixture becomes fragrant
and changes colour. Add the tom yum
paste and stir briefly before gradually
adding the coconut milk and stock,
stirring constantly to mix the paste
into the liquid. Add the sugar and
½ teaspoon salt and bring to the boil.
Reduce the heat to low and simmer
for 10 minutes. Add the beans and
carrot, and cook for 5 minutes more.
Skim any fat from the top.
2 Add the noodles, sprouts and beef
just before serving, and cook just long
enough to heat through. Garnish with
coriander leaves. This dish is best
eaten from a large, deep bowl with
chopsticks and a soup spoon.

NUTRITION PER SERVE
Protein 20 g; Fat 58 g; Carbohydrate 65 g;
Dietary Fibre 8.5 g; Cholesterol 25 mg;
3599 kJ (860 Cal)

Peel the galangal and finely grate with a wooden grater.

Wearing protective gloves, remove the seeds and finely chop the chillies.

Use a sharp knife to cut the carrot into julienne strips.

Stir in the onion, ginger, galangal, garlic, lemongrass, chilli and macadamias.

VEGETABLE DUMPLINGS

Preparation time: 40 minutes +
    15 minutes soaking
Total cooking time: 20 minutes
Makes 24

8 dried Chinese mushrooms
1 tablespoon oil
2 teaspoons finely chopped fresh
    ginger
2 garlic cloves, crushed
100 g (3¹/₂ oz) Chinese chives,
    chopped
100 g (3¹/₂ oz) water spinach, cut into
    1 cm (¹/₂ inch) lengths
¹/₄ cup (60 ml/2 fl oz) chicken stock
2 tablespoons oyster sauce
1 tablespoon cornflour
1 teaspoon soy sauce
1 teaspoon rice wine
¹/₄ cup (45 g/1¹/₂ oz) water chestnuts,
    chopped
chilli sauce, to serve

WRAPPERS
200 g (6¹/₂ oz) wheat starch
    (see NOTE)
1 teaspoon cornflour
oil, for kneading

1 Place the mushrooms in a bowl and soak in 2 cups (500 ml/16 fl oz) hot water for 15 minutes. Finely chop the mushroom caps.
2 Heat the oil in a frying pan over high heat, add the ginger, garlic and a pinch of salt and white pepper and cook for 30 seconds. Add the chives and spinach and cook for 1 minute.
3 Combine the stock, oyster sauce, cornflour, soy sauce and rice wine, and add to the spinach mixture along with the water chestnuts and mushrooms. Cook for 1–2 minutes, or until the

mixture thickens, them remove from the heat and cool completely.
4 To make the wrappers, combine the wheat starch and cornflour in a bowl. Make a well in the centre and add ³/₄ cup (185 ml/6 fl oz) boiling water, a little at a time, while bringing the mixture together with your hands. When it is combined, immediately knead it, using lightly oiled hands until the dough forms a shiny ball.
5 Keeping the dough covered with a cloth while you work, pick walnut-sized pieces from the dough, and using well-oiled hands, squash them between the palms of your hands then roll out as thinly as possible into circles no larger than 10 cm (4 inches)

in diameter. Place 1 tablespoon of the filling in the centre of the circle. Pinch the edges of the wrapper together to enclose the filling and form a tight ball.
6 Fill a wok or saucepan one-third full of water and bring to the boil. Put the dumplings in a bamboo steamer lined with baking paper, leaving a gap between each one. Cover and steam for 7–8 minutes. Serve with chilli sauce.

NUTRITION PER DUMPLING
Protein 0.5 g; Fat 1 g; Carbohydrate 8.5 g;
Dietary Fibre 0.5 g; Cholesterol 0 mg; 185 kJ
(45 Cal)

NOTE: Wheat starch is a very fine white powder similar to cornflour.

Use lightly oiled hands to roll the dumpling wrapper dough into a ball.

Roll out the small pieces of dough into flat rounds, taking care not to tear them.

Pinch the edges of the wrapper together so that the filling is enclosed.

CHICKEN SATAY WITH PEANUT SAUCE

Preparation time: 40 minutes
+ 30 minutes marinating
Total cooking time: 15–20 minutes
Serves 4

500 g (1 lb) chicken thigh fillets,
   trimmed
1 onion, roughly chopped
2 stems lemon grass, white part only,
   thinly sliced
4 cloves garlic
2 red chillies, chopped
2 teaspoons ground coriander
1 teaspoon ground cumin
1/2 teaspoon salt
1 tablespoon soy sauce
1/4 cup (60 ml/2 fl oz) oil
1 tablespoon soft brown sugar
cucumber slices, to serve
chopped roasted peanuts, to serve

PEANUT SAUCE
1/2 cup (125 g/4 oz) crunchy peanut
   butter
1 cup (250 ml/8 fl oz) coconut milk
1–2 tablespoons sweet chilli sauce
1 tablespoon soy sauce
2 teaspoons lemon juice

1 Soak 20 wooden skewers in cold water for 30 minutes. Cut the chicken into thick flattish strips. Thread a strip of chicken onto each skewer, flattening it on the skewer.
2 Process the onion, lemon grass, garlic, chilli, coriander, cumin, salt and soy sauce in a food processor, in short bursts, until smooth, adding a little oil to assist the processing. Spread the lemon grass mixture over the chicken, cover and refrigerate for 30 minutes.
3 To make the peanut sauce, put the peanut butter, coconut milk, sweet chilli sauce, soy sauce and lemon juice in a heavy-based pan with 1/2 cup (125 ml/4 fl oz) water. Stir over low heat until the mixture boils. Remove from the heat. The sauce will thicken on standing.
4 Heat a chargrill or barbecue flatplate until very hot and brush with the remaining oil. Cook the chicken for 2–3 minutes on each side, sprinkling with a little oil and brown sugar (this

Thread one chicken strip onto each skewer, flattening it out on the skewer.

Add a little oil to the lemon grass paste to assist the processing.

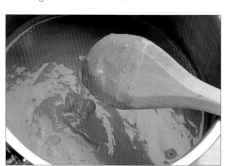
The peanut sauce will thicken when it has been standing.

During cooking, sprinkle the chicken with oil and brown sugar.

will help produce a lovely flavour and colour). Serve topped with the peanut sauce and garnished with the cucumber and peanuts. Serve the remaining peanut sauce as a dipping sauce.

NUTRITION PER SERVE
Protein 40 g; Fat 45 g; Carbohydrate 14 g;
Dietary Fibre 6 g; Cholesterol 60 mg;
2600 kJ (620 cal)

WON TON NOODLE SOUP

Preparation time: 25 minutes
Total cooking time: 25 minutes
Serves 4

70 g (2¼ oz) raw prawns
70 g (2¼ oz) veal mince
3 tablespoons soy sauce
1 tablespoon finely chopped spring onion
1 tablespoon finely chopped water chestnuts
1 teaspoon finely chopped fresh ginger
2 cloves garlic, finely chopped

24 gow gee wrappers
5 cups (1.25 litres) chicken stock
2 tablespoons mirin
500 g (1 lb) baby bok choy, finely shredded
8 spring onions, sliced

1 Peel, devein and finely chop the prawns. Mix with the veal mince, 2 teaspoons soy sauce, spring onion, water chestnuts, ginger and garlic. Lay the round wrappers out on a work surface and place a teaspoon of mixture in the middle of each.
2 Moisten the edges of the wrappers and bring up the sides to form a pouch. Pinch together to seal. Cook in batches in a large pan of rapidly boiling water for 4–5 minutes. Drain and divide among soup bowls.
3 Bring the stock, remaining soy sauce and mirin to the boil in a large suacepan. Add the bok choy, cover and simmer for 2 minutes, or until the bok choy has just wilted. Add the sliced spring onion and season. Ladle the stock, bok choy and spring onion over the won tons.

NUTRITION PER SERVE
Protein 10 g; Fat 5 g; Carbohydrate 30 g;
Dietary Fibre 5 g; Cholesterol 25 mg;
760 kJ (180 cal)

Peel the prawns and devein them before chopping them finely.

Bring the sides of the wrappers up around the filling and pinch to seal.

Add the finely shredded bok choy to the pan and simmer until just wilted.

TOM KHA GAI (CHICKEN AND COCONUT SOUP)

Preparation time: 20 minutes
Total cooking time: 20 minutes
Serves 4

5 cm (2 inch) piece galangal (see Hint)
2 cups (500 ml/16 fl oz) coconut milk
1 cup (250 ml/8 fl oz) chicken stock
3 chicken breast fillets, cut into
    thin strips
1–2 teaspoons finely chopped red
    chilli

2 tablespoons fish sauce
1 teaspoon soft brown sugar
1/4 cup (7 g/1/4 oz) fresh coriander
    leaves
fresh coriander sprigs, to serve

1 Peel the galangal and cut it into thin slices. Combine the galangal, coconut milk and stock in a medium pan. Bring to the boil and simmer, uncovered, over low heat for 10 minutes, stirring occasionally.
2 Add the chicken strips and chilli to the pan and simmer for 8 minutes.
3 Stir in the fish sauce and brown sugar. Add the coriander leaves and serve immediately, garnished with the fresh coriander sprigs.

NUTRITION PER SERVE
Protein 40 g; Fat 30 g; Carbohydrate 6.5 g;
Dietary Fibre 2.5 g; Cholesterol 83 mg;
1876 kJ (448 cal)

HINT: If fresh galangal is not available, you can use 5 large slices of dried galangal instead. Prepare by soaking the slices in a little boiling water for 10 minutes and then cutting them into shreds. Add the soaking liquid to the chicken stock to make 1 cup (250 ml/ 8 fl oz) and use it in the recipe.

Break the galangal so you have a piece measuring about 5 cm (2 inches).

Add the chicken strips and chilli to the simmering coconut milk mixture.

Just before serving, add the fresh coriander leaves to the pan.

CHINESE BARBECUED PORK PIES

Preparation time: 35 minutes
  + 1 hour refrigeration
Total cooking time: 45 minutes
Makes 4

2 tablespoons cornflour
1/4 cup (60 ml/ 2 fl oz) oyster sauce
1/4 cup (60 ml/2 fl oz) rice wine
2 tablespoons kecap manis
2 tablespoons lime juice
1 tablespoon grated fresh ginger
1/2 teaspoon ground white pepper
400 g (13 oz) Chinese barbecued
    pork, cut into 1 cm (1/2 inch) dice
150 g (5 oz) snow peas, sliced
2 cups (100 g/3 1/2 oz) thinly sliced
    Chinese cabbage
375 g (12 oz) shortcrust pastry
375 g (12 oz) puff pastry
milk, for brushing
1 teaspoon sesame seeds

1 Preheat the oven to moderate 180°C (350°F/Gas 4). Grease four 11 cm (4 1/2 inch) top, 9 cm (3 1/2 inch) base and 3 cm (1 1/4 inch) deep metal pie dishes. Mix the cornflour with 2 tablespoons water. Heat a large frying pan over low heat and add the oyster sauce, rice wine, kecap manis; lime juice, ginger, white pepper and the cornflour mixture. Simmer for 2 minutes, or until very thick. Add the pork, snow peas and cabbage. Cook, stirring, for 5 minutes. Cool, then refrigerate for 1 hour, or until cold.
2 Meanwhile, roll out the shortcrust pastry between two sheets of baking paper until it is 3 mm (1/8 inch) thick. Cut out four 16 cm (6 1/2 inch) rounds. Line the pie dishes with the pastry, then refrigerate.

3 When the filling is cold, fill the pastry shells. Roll out the puff pastry between the baking paper to 3 mm (1/8 inch) thick and cut out four rounds large enough to cover the tops of the pie dishes. Cover the pies with the puff pastry rounds and trim any excess. Use a fork to seal the edges and prick a few holes in the top. Brush the lids with milk, sprinkle with sesame seeds, and bake for 35 minutes, or until golden.

NUTRITION PER PIE
Protein 35 g; Fat 60.5 g; Carbohydrate 86 g; Dietary Fibre 7 g; Cholesterol 112.5 mg; 4360 kJ (1040 Cal)

Add the pork, snow peas and cabbage and cook, stirring, for 5 minutes.

Cut four 16 cm (6 1/2 inch) rounds of shortcrust pastry and use them to line the pie dishes.

Cut rounds from the puff pastry and cover the tops of the pies.

HOT AND SOUR LIME SOUP WITH BEEF

Preparation time: 20 minutes
Total cooking time: 35 minutes
Serves 4

1 litre beef stock
2 stems lemon grass, white part
    only, halved
3 cloves garlic, halved
2.5 cm x 2.5 cm (1 inch x 1 inch)
    piece fresh ginger, sliced
95 g (3 oz) fresh coriander, leaves
    and stalks separated
2 1.5 cm x 4 cm (5/8 inch x 1 1/2 inch)
    strips lime rind
2 star anise
3 small fresh red chillies, seeded
    and finely chopped
4 spring onions, thinly sliced on
    the diagonal
500 g (1 lb) fillet steak, trimmed
2 tablespoons fish sauce
1 tablespoon grated palm sugar
2 tablespoons lime juice
fresh coriander leaves, extra,
    to garnish

1 Place the stock, lemon grass, garlic, ginger, coriander stalks, rind, star anise, 1 teaspoon chopped chilli, half the spring onion, and 1 litre water in a saucepan. Bring to the boil and simmer, covered, for 25 minutes. Strain and return the liquid to the pan.
2 Heat a chargrill pan until very hot. Brush with olive oil and sear the steak on both sides until browned on the outside, but very rare in the centre.
3 Reheat the soup, adding the fish sauce and palm sugar. Season and add the lime juice to taste (you may want more than 2 tablespoons)—you should achieve a hot and sour flavour.

4 Add the remaining spring onion and the chopped coriander leaves to the soup. Slice the beef across the grain into thin strips. Curl the strips into a decorative pattern, then place in four deep serving bowls. Pour the soup over the beef and garnish with the remaining chilli and coriander leaves.

NUTRITION PER SERVE
Protein 31 g; Fat 7 g; Carbohydrate 7 g; Dietary Fibre 0.5 g; Cholesterol 84 mg; 900 kJ (215 Cal)

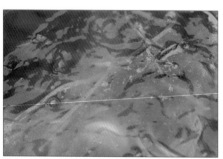

Bring the soup to the boil, then reduce the heat and simmer for 25 minutes.

Brown the fillet steak on a hot, lightly oiled chargrill pan.

Gently curl the thin strips of beef into a decorative pattern.

SEAFOOD RAVIOLI IN GINGERY SOUP

Preparation time: 30 minutes
Total cooking time: 20 minutes
Serves 4

8 raw prawns
1 carrot, chopped
1 onion, chopped
1 celery stick, chopped
3 spring onions, thinly sliced
6 cm (2¹/2 inch) piece fresh ginger,
    thinly shredded
1 tablespoon mirin
1 teaspoon kecap manis
1 tablespoon soy sauce
4 large scallops
100 g (3¹/2 oz) boneless white fish fillet
1 egg white
200 g (6¹/2 oz) round gow gee
    wrappers
¹/3 cup (10 g/¹/4 oz) fresh coriander
    leaves

1 To make the soup, peel the prawns, reserve 4 for the ravioli filling and chop the rest into small pieces and reserve. Put the prawn heads and shells in a large pan, cook over high heat until starting to brown, then cover with 1 litre water. Add the carrot, onion and celery, bring to the boil, reduce the heat and simmer for 10 minutes. Strain and discard the prawn heads, shells and vegetables. Return the stock to a clean pan and add the spring onion, ginger, mirin, kecap manis and soy sauce. Set aside.
2 To make the ravioli, chop the whole reserved prawns with the scallops and fish in a food processor until smooth. Add enough egg white to bind. Lay half the gow gee wrappers on a work surface and place a rounded teaspoon

of filling in the centre of each. Brush the edges with water. Top each with another wrapper and press the edges to seal, eliminating air bubbles as you go. Trim with a fluted cutter. Cover with plastic wrap.
3 Bring a large pan of water to the boil. Meanwhile, heat the stock and leave simmering. Just prior to serving, drop a few ravioli at a time into the boiling water. Cook for 2 minutes, remove with a slotted spoon and

divide among heated bowls. Cook the chopped reserved prawns in the same water for 2 minutes; drain. Pour the hot stock over the ravioli and serve, sprinkled with the chopped cooked prawns and coriander leaves.

NUTRITION PER SERVE
Protein 17 g; Fat 7 g; Carbohydrate 65 g;
Dietary Fibre 4.5 g; Cholesterol 125 mg;
1765 kJ (420 Cal)

Stir the prawn heads and shells in a pan over high heat until lightly browned.

Brush the edge of one wrapper with water, then cover with another.

Cook each batch of ravioli for 2 minutes, then remove with a slotted spoon.

CHICKEN CURRY LAKSA

Preparation time: 30 minutes
Total cooking time: 25 minutes
Serves 4

500 g (1 lb) chicken breast fillets
1 large onion, roughly chopped
5 cm (2 inch) piece ginger, chopped
8 cm (3 inch) piece galangal, peeled and chopped
1 stem lemon grass, white part only, roughly chopped
2 cloves garlic
1 red chilli, seeded and chopped
2 teaspoons oil
2 tablespoons mild curry paste
2 cups (500 ml/16 fl oz) chicken stock
60 g (2 oz) rice vermicelli
50 g (1³/₄ oz) dried egg noodles
400 ml (13 fl oz) light coconut milk
10 snow peas, halved
3 spring onions, finely chopped
1 cup (90 g/3 oz) bean sprouts
¹/₂ cup (15 g/¹/₂ oz) fresh coriander leaves

1 Cut the chicken into bite-sized cubes. Process the onion, ginger, galangal, lemon grass, garlic and chilli in a food processor until finely chopped. Add the oil and process until the mixture is a paste-like consistency.

Spoon into a large wok, add the curry paste and stir over low heat for 1–2 minutes, or until aromatic. Take care not to burn the mixture.
2 Increase the heat to medium, add the chicken and stir for 2 minutes, or until the chicken is well coated. Stir in the chicken stock and mix well. Bring slowly to the boil, then simmer for 10 minutes, or until the chicken is cooked through.
3 Meanwhile, cut the vermicelli into shorter lengths using scissors. Cook the vermicelli and egg noodles separately in large pans of boiling water for 5 minutes each. Drain and rinse under cold water.
4 Just prior to serving, add the light coconut milk and snow peas to the chicken mixture and heat through. To serve, divide the vermicelli and noodles among four warmed serving bowls. Pour the hot laksa over the top and garnish with the spring onion, bean sprouts and coriander leaves.

NUTRITION PER SERVE
Protein 30 g; Fat 8 g; Carbohydrate 4.5 g;
Dietary Fibre 3 g; Cholesterol 65 mg;
945 kJ (225 cal)

HINT: If you prefer a more fiery laksa, use a medium or hot brand of curry paste or increase the amount of chilli.

Stir the curry paste into the onion mixture, over low heat, until aromatic.

Just before serving, stir the coconut milk into the chicken mixture until heated.

PRAWN SPRING ROLLS

Preparation time: 50 minutes
Total cooking time: 4 minutes
Makes about 18

50 g (1³/₄ oz) rice vermicelli
2 spring onions
1 Lebanese cucumber, peeled
1 carrot
24 cooked prawns, peeled and
    chopped
2 tablespoons chopped roasted
    unsalted peanuts
2 Chinese mushrooms, soaked,
    chopped finely
¹/₂ lettuce, finely shredded
¹/₂ cup (25 g/³/₄ oz) chopped
    fresh mint
50 g (1³/₄ oz) bean sprouts
375 g (12 oz) rice paper rounds,
    21 cm (8¹/₂ inch) diameter

DIPPING SAUCE
2 tablespoons caster sugar
2 tablespoons fish sauce
2 tablespoons lime juice
1 tablespoon rice vinegar or white
    vinegar
1 spring onion, finely chopped
1 small red chilli, seeded and finely
    chopped
1 clove garlic, crushed

1 Put the vermicelli in a large bowl, cover with boiling water and leave for 1–2 minutes, or until soft. Rinse under cold water, drain, chop roughly with scissors and put in a bowl.
2 Very finely shred the spring onions, cucumber and carrot into 5 cm (2 inch) strips. Blanch the carrot for 1 minute, drain and cool. Add the carrot, spring onion and cucumber to the cooled vermicelli with the prawns, peanuts, mushrooms, lettuce, mint and sprouts. Using your hands, toss until the mixture is well combined.
3 For each spring roll, soften a rice paper in a bowl of warm water for 10–20 seconds. Lay it on a tea towel and place 3 tablespoons of filling in the centre. Fold in the sides and roll up into a parcel. Seal the edges by brushing with a little water. Place on a serving platter and cover with a damp cloth while you make the rest.

4 To make the dipping sauce, combine the sugar and 2 tablespoons warm water in a small bowl and stir until the sugar dissolves. Add the remaining ingredients and stir well. Serve with the spring rolls.

NUTRITION PER SPRING ROLL
Protein 5 g; Fat 1 g; Carbohydrate 9 g;
Dietary Fibre 1 g; Cholesterol 25 mg;
265 kJ (65 Cal)

The spring onion, cucumber and carrot should be cut into short, fine strips.

Soften one sheet of rice paper at a time in a bowl of warm water.

Put the filling in the centre of the rice paper, then roll and fold into a parcel.

TERIYAKI CHICKEN WINGS

Preparation time: 15 minutes
+ 3 hours marinating
Total cooking time: 15 minutes
Serves 4

8 chicken wings
1/4 cup (60 ml/2 fl oz) soy sauce
2 tablespoons sherry
2 teaspoons grated fresh ginger
1 clove garlic, crushed
1 tablespoon honey

1 Pat the chicken wings dry with paper towels. Trim any excess fat from the wings, and tuck the tips under to form a triangle.

2 Place the wings in a shallow non-metal dish. Combine the soy sauce, sherry, ginger, garlic and honey in a jug, and mix well. Pour the mixture over the chicken wings. Refrigerate, covered, for several hours or overnight. Lightly brush two sheets of aluminium foil with oil. Place 4 wings in a single layer on each piece of foil and wrap completely.

3 Preheat a barbecue grill or flatplate to high. Cook the parcels on the hot barbecue for 10 minutes. Remove the parcels from the heat and unwrap. Place the wings directly on a lightly greased grill for 3 minutes, or until brown. Turn the wings frequently and brush with any remaining marinade.

NUTRITION PER SERVE
Protein 43 g; Fat 4.5 g; Carbohydrate 6 g;
Dietary Fibre 0 g; Cholesterol 95 mg;
998 kJ (238 Cal)

Tuck the tips of the chicken wings under to form a triangle.

Place four chicken wings on each piece of foil and wrap completely.

Place the wings directly on a lightly greased grill and cook until brown.

SESAME AND WASABI-CRUSTED TUNA CUBES

Preparation time: 10 minutes
Total cooking time: 5 minutes
Makes about 40

GINGER AND SOY DIPPING SAUCE
2 cm x 2 cm (³⁄₄ inch x ³⁄₄ inch) piece
    fresh ginger, cut into julienne strips
2 tablespoons Japanese soy sauce
2 tablespoons mirin
1 teaspoon wasabi paste
¼ teaspoon sesame oil

TUNA CUBES
600 g (1¼ lb) fresh tuna steaks
1 teaspoon wasabi powder
⅓ cup (50 g/1³⁄₄ oz) black sesame
    seeds
¼ cup (60 ml/2 fl oz) oil

1 To make the dipping sauce, place the ginger, Japanese soy sauce, mirin, wasabi paste and sesame oil in a small bowl and mix together well. Set aside until needed.
2 Cut the tuna into 2 cm (³⁄₄ inch) cubes using a very sharp knife. Put the tuna cubes in a large bowl. Add the combined wasabi powder and black sesame seeds to the bowl and toss well until the tuna cubes are evenly coated in powder and seeds.
3 Heat a wok over high heat, add half the oil and swirl to coat. Add half the tuna and cook, tossing gently, for 1–2 minutes, or until lightly golden on the outside but still pink in the middle. Drain on crumpled paper towels and repeat with the remaining oil and tuna. Arrange the tuna cubes on a platter with the dipping sauce in the centre and serve with toothpicks so that your guests can pick up the cubes.

NUTRITION PER PIECE
Protein 4 g; Fat 3 g; Carbohydrate 0 g; Dietary Fibre 0 g; Cholesterol 5.5 mg; 175 kJ (40 Cal)

THINK AHEAD: The dipping sauce will keep in the refrigerator for up to 1 week, but the tuna is best if cooked no more than 3 hours in advance.

VARIATION: The tuna cubes are also very nice served with a chilli and lime dipping sauce instead of the ginger and soy one in the recipe. To make the dipping sauce, dissolve 2 tablespoons grated palm sugar or soft brown sugar in a small bowl with 2 tablespoons lime juice. Add 1 tablespoon fish sauce and 1 seeded and finely chopped fresh red bird's eye chilli. Mix together well. This sauce will keep in the refrigerator for 2–3 days.

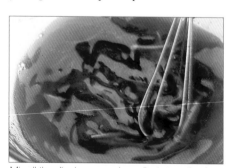

Mix all the dipping sauce ingredients together in a small bowl.

Use a sharp knife to cut the tuna steaks into even 2 cm (³⁄₄ inch) cubes.

Coat the tuna cubes in the black sesame seeds and wasabi powder.

THAI CHICKEN BALLS

Preparation time: 20 minutes
Total cooking time: 40 minutes
Serves 6

1 kg (2 lb) chicken mince
1 cup (80 g/2¾ oz) fresh
　breadcrumbs
4 spring onions, sliced
1 tablespoon ground coriander
1 cup (50 g/1¾ oz) chopped fresh
　coriander
¼ cup (60 ml/2 fl oz) sweet chilli sauce

1–2 tablespoons lemon juice
oil, for shallow frying

1 Preheat the oven to moderately hot 200°C (400°F/Gas 6). Mix the mince and breadcrumbs in a large bowl.
2 Add the spring onion, ground and fresh coriander, chilli sauce and lemon juice, and mix well. Using damp hands, form the mixture into even balls that are either small enough to eat with your fingers.
3 Heat the oil in a deep frying pan, and shallow-fry the chicken balls in batches over high heat until browned

all over. Place the chicken balls on a baking tray and bake until cooked through. (The small chicken balls will take 5 minutes to cook and the larger ones will take 10–15 minutes.) This mixture also makes a delicious filling for sausage rolls.

NUTRITION PER SERVE
Protein 34.5 g; Fat 18.5 g; Carbohydrate 13 g;
Dietary Fibre 2 g; Cholesterol 150 mg;
1475 kJ (350 Cal)

Mix the spring onion, coriander, chilli sauce and lemon juice into the chicken mixture.

With damp hands, form the mixture into evenly shaped balls.

Fry the chicken balls in oil until they are browned on both sides.

noodles & rice

Noodles & Rice

Noodles and rice, the perfect accompaniments to stir-fries, come in an exciting array of types, colours, shapes and sizes. Some are pre-cooked and just need to be heated.

NOODLES

Fresh egg noodles

These are made from egg and wheat flour and need to be cooked in boiling water before use. Refrigerate until you are ready to use them.

Fresh rice noodles

Available thick or thin, or as a sheet or roll which can be cut to a desired width, these white rice noodles are steamed and lightly oiled before packing, and so are ready to use. They must be brought to room temperature before use, as they harden during refrigeration.

Hokkien noodles

These yellow, thick noodles are made from wheat flour and egg. They are pre-cooked and lightly oiled, so are ready to use. Refrigerate until ready to use, then roughly separate with your fingers. They can be soaked in hot water to soften up before stir-frying.

Instant noodles

Different brands of dried instant noodles are stocked in supermarkets. They are made from wheat flour and are very quick to prepare.

Rice sticks (dried)

Resembling fettuccine, these flat, translucent noodles are often used in stir-fries. They are sold packaged in bundles. Soak them in warm water before using.

Rice vermicelli (dried)

Sold packaged in blocks, these thin, translucent noodles need to be soaked in boiling water, or boiled until tender and thoroughly drained before use.

Soba noodles

A northern Japanese speciality made from buckwheat and/or wheat flour, these are eaten hot or cold. They absorb flavour well and are good with dishes that have a strongly flavoured dressing.

Udon noodles

White, round or flat Japanese wheat flour noodles, these are available either dried or fresh. They plump up to become slippery, fat noodles with a unique texture.

Noodles, from left to right, top row: fresh egg, Hokkien, dried rice sticks, soba.
Bottom row: fresh rice, instant, rice vermicelli, udon.

RICE

Basmati

With long fragrant grains which remain separate when cooked, this rice is very aromatic and complements Asian flavours well. Basmati rice is grown in India on the foothills of the Himalayas and is now popular throughout the world. Traditionally served with curries, where saffron is added to give the dish colour and flavour.

Brown rice

Brown rice has not had the bran removed and is therefore valued for its nutritional properties. Cooking is a lot slower than for white rice as it takes a considerable time for the water to break through the bran layer.

Jasmine rice

This is a long-grain, fragrant white rice used throughout Southeast Asia. It is usually steamed, or cooked using the absorption method. Jasmine rice is served as an accompaniment to all Thai meals.

Long-grain white rice

This is the rice which is chosen above all others by the Chinese—perhaps stemming from Confucius' insistence on eating the whitest rice available. It is grown in the monsoon region of Southeast Asia and is often referred to as 'water rice'. Long-grain white rice has been processed to remove the outer hull and bran, then polished until it is white and glossy.

Wild rice

Wild rice has a nutty flavour and a high protein content. These long dark brown grains come from an aquatic grass—so wild rice is not really a rice at all, but the grain of a water grass native to the great lakes of North America. Grown originally by the Chippewa Indians and harvested by hand, it is now farmed by machine. The grains have a delicious flavour and a distinguishable chewy texture. Wild rice requires thorough washing before use. It can be bought in small packets and is expensive compared to other rices. These days it is available mixed with brown rice and sold as a wild rice blend, which makes it cheaper.

Rice, from top: basmati, brown, jasmine, long-grain white, wild.

SAVOURY RICE AND EGGS

Preparation time: 20 minutes
Total cooking time: 12 minutes
Serves 4

2 tablespoons ghee (see NOTE) or oil
1 onion, finely chopped
1/2 red capsicum, finely chopped
10 spring onions, thinly sliced
2–3 small red chillies, seeded and
    finely chopped
2–3 cloves garlic, finely chopped
1 tablespoon grated fresh ginger
125 g (4 oz) Chinese barbecued pork,
    finely chopped
6 eggs, lightly beaten

4 cups (740 g/1 1/2 lb) cold cooked
    jasmine rice
1–2 teaspoons seasoning sauce
1/3 cup (20 g/3/4 oz) chopped fresh
    coriander
onion flakes, to garnish

1 Heat the wok until very hot, add
the ghee and swirl it around to coat
the side. Stir-fry the onion, capsicum,
spring onion, chilli, garlic and
ginger over medium–high heat for
2–3 minutes, or until the vegetables
are cooked but not brown. Add the
barbecued pork and toss to combine.
2 Reduce the heat, then pour in the
beaten eggs. Season well with salt and
pepper. Gently stir the egg mixture

until it is creamy and almost set.
Add the rice and gently stir-fry to
incorporate all the ingredients and
heat the mixture through.
3 Sprinkle with the seasoning sauce
and stir in the coriander. Serve the
savoury rice immediately, sprinkled
with onion flakes.

NUTRITION PER SERVE
Protein 15 g; Fat 20 g; Carbohydrate 60 g;
Dietary Fibre 3.5 g; Cholesterol 295 mg;
2105 kJ (500 Cal)

NOTE: Ghee is a form of clarified
butter. It is the main type of fat used
in Indian cooking and is available in
most supermarkets.

Cut the Chinese barbecued pork into slices, then
chop it finely.

Add the barbecued pork to the onion mixture and
toss to combine.

Add the egg, season well and stir gently until the
mixture is creamy.

CHICKEN CHOW MEIN

Preparation time: 25 minutes
+ 1 hour marinating
Total cooking time: 25 minutes
Serves 4–6

500 g (1 lb) chicken thigh fillets,
   cut into small cubes
1 tablespoon cornflour
2 tablespoons soy sauce
1 tablespoon oyster sauce
2 teaspoons sugar
oil, for cooking
2 onions, thinly sliced
2 cloves garlic, finely chopped
1 tablespoon finely chopped fresh
   ginger
1 green capsicum, cubed
2 celery sticks, diagonally sliced
8 spring onions, cut into short pieces
100 g (3½ oz) mushrooms, thinly
   sliced
½ cup (80 g/2¾ oz) water chestnuts,
   thinly sliced
2 teaspoons cornflour, extra
1 tablespoon sherry

½ cup (125 ml/4 fl oz) chicken stock
1 tablespoon soy sauce, extra
90 g (3 oz) Chinese cabbage, finely
   shredded
200 g (6½ oz) ready-prepared fried
   noodles

1 In a glass or ceramic bowl, combine the chicken with the cornflour, soy sauce, oyster sauce and sugar. Cover and refrigerate for 1 hour.
2 Heat the wok until very hot, add 1 tablespoon of the oil and swirl it around to coat the side. Stir-fry the chicken in two batches over high heat for 4–5 minutes, or until cooked. Add oil between batches. Remove all the chicken from the wok and set it aside.
3 Reheat the wok, add 1 tablespoon of the oil and stir-fry the onion over medium–high heat for 3–4 minutes, or until the onion is slightly softened. Add the garlic, ginger, capsicum, celery, spring onion, mushrooms and water chestnuts to the wok. Stir-fry over high heat for 3–4 minutes.
4 Combine the extra cornflour with the sherry, chicken stock and soy

sauce. Add to the wok and bring to the boil. Simmer for 1–2 minutes, or until the sauce thickens slightly. Stir in the cabbage and cook, covered, for 1–2 minutes, or until the cabbage is just wilted. Return the chicken to the wok and toss until heated through. Season with salt and pepper. Arrange the noodles around the edge of a large platter and spoon the chicken mixture into the centre. Serve immediately.

NUTRITION PER SERVE (6)
Protein 25 g; Fat 8.5 g; Carbohydrate 20 g;
Dietary Fibre 4 g; Cholesterol 55 mg;
1110 kJ (265 Cal)

Combine the cornflour, sherry, stock and soy sauce, and pour into the wok.

MEE GORENG

Preparation time: 45 minutes
Total cooking time: 10 minutes
Serves 4

1 large onion, finely chopped
2 cloves garlic, finely chopped
2 red chillies, seeded and finely
    chopped
2 cm (3/4 inch) piece fresh ginger,
    grated
oil, for cooking
350 g (11 oz) Hokkien noodles, gently
    pulled apart (see NOTE)
500 g (1 lb) peeled raw prawns
250 g (8 oz) rump steak, finely sliced
4 spring onions, chopped
1 large carrot, cut into matchsticks
2 celery sticks, cut into matchsticks
1 tablespoon kecap manis
1 tablespoon soy sauce
1 tablespoon tomato sauce

1 Combine the onion, garlic, chilli and ginger in a small food processor or mortar and pestle. Process in short bursts, or pound, until a paste forms, adding a little oil to help the grinding, if necessary.

2 Heat the wok until very hot, add 1 tablespoon of the oil and swirl it around to coat the side. Stir-fry the noodles until plump and warmed through. Remove to a serving plate; cover to keep warm.

3 Add another tablespoon of oil to the wok and stir-fry the paste until golden. Add the prawns, steak, spring onion, carrot and celery and stir-fry for 2–3 minutes. Add the kecap manis, soy and tomato sauces and season well with salt and pepper. Serve immediately over the noodles.

NUTRITION PER SERVE
Protein 43 g; Fat 17 g; Carbohydrate 14 g;
Dietary Fibre 2.5 g; Cholesterol 230 mg;
1600 kJ (380 cal)

NOTE: Hokkien noodles are thick yellow noodles that have already been cooked and are ready to use. If they are not available, you can use dried egg noodles, but they must be cooked and drained well beforehand.

Gently prise apart the Hokkien noodles before heating in the wok.

Stir-fry the noodles in the wok until they are warmed through.

Heat the oil in the wok and stir-fry the paste mixture until it is golden.

Add the kecap manis, soy and tomato sauces to the steak, prawns and vegetables.

CHILLI-CRUSTED CHICKEN NOODLES

Preparation time: 25 minutes
Total cooking time: 20 minutes
Serves 4–6

1½ teaspoons chilli powder
3 tablespoons cornflour
1½ teaspoons salt
2 tablespoons oil
350 g (12 oz) chicken thigh fillets, sliced
4 spring onions, sliced
1 carrot, sliced
1 celery stick, sliced

2 tablespoons mirin or sherry
500 g (1 lb) Hokkien noodles, gently pulled apart
2 tablespoons oyster sauce
250 g (8 oz) baby bok choy, washed, trimmed, leaves separated

1 Combine the chilli powder, cornflour and salt and mix well. Heat the oil in a wok over high heat. Coat the chicken strips in the cornflour mix and stir-fry in batches for 3 minutes each batch, or until golden. Drain on paper towels and remove all the chicken from the wok.

2 Reheat the wok over medium heat. Add the spring onion, carrot and celery and stir-fry for 1 minute. Add the mirin and the noodles, tossing well until the vegetables have softened.

3 Add the oyster sauce and 2 tablespoons water; cover and steam for 2–4 minutes, or until the noodles are tender.

4 Add the chicken and bok choy and toss well. Cover and steam for 30 seconds only. Serve immediately.

NUTRITION PER SERVE (6)
Protein 15 g; Fat 9 g; Carbohydrate 30 g;
Dietary Fibre 3 g; Cholesterol 40 mg;
1165 kJ (275 cal)

Gently pull apart the Hokkien noodles before you cook them.

Coat the chicken in the mixture of cornflour, chilli powder and salt.

Stir-fry the chicken in small batches so that the wok doesn't overcrowd and cool down.

SINGAPORE NOODLES

Preparation time: 20 minutes
Total cooking time: 10 minutes
Serves 4–6

150 g (5 oz) dried rice vermicelli
oil, for cooking
250 g (8 oz) Chinese barbecued pork,
 cut into small pieces
250 g (8 oz) peeled raw prawns, cut
 into small pieces
2 tablespoons Madras curry powder
2 cloves garlic, crushed
100 g (3½ oz) shiitake mushrooms,
 thinly sliced

1 onion, thinly sliced
100 g (3½ oz) green beans, thinly
 sliced on the diagonal
1 tablespoon soy sauce
4 spring onions, thinly sliced on the
 diagonal

1 Place the vermicelli in a large bowl, cover with boiling water and soak for 5 minutes. Drain well and spread out on a clean tea towel to dry.
2 Heat the wok until very hot, add 1 tablespoon of the oil and swirl it around to coat the side. Stir-fry the barbecued pork and the prawn pieces in batches over high heat. Remove from the wok and set aside.

3 Reheat the wok, add 2 tablespoons of the oil and stir-fry the curry powder and garlic for 1–2 minutes, or until fragrant. Add the mushrooms and onion and stir-fry over medium heat for 2–3 minutes, or until the onion and mushrooms are soft.
4 Return the pork and prawns to the wok, add the beans and 2 teaspoons water, and toss to combine. Add the drained noodles, soy sauce and spring onion. Toss well and serve.

NUTRITION PER SERVE (6)
Protein 10 g; Fat 7.5 g; Carbohydrate 25 g;
Dietary Fibre 3 g; Cholesterol 60 mg;
905 kJ (215 cal)

Cut the barbecued pork into slices, then into small pieces.

Put the vermicelli in a heatproof bowl, cover with boiling water and leave to soak.

Stir-fry the curry powder and garlic in the oil until the mixture is fragrant.

FRESH RICE NOODLES WITH BEEF

Preparation time: 10 minutes
  + 30 minutes marinating
Total cooking time: 15 minutes
Serves 4–6

2 cloves garlic, crushed
2 teaspoons chopped fresh ginger
1 tablespoon oyster sauce
2 teaspoons soy sauce
500 g (1 lb) beef, thinly sliced
oil, for cooking

1 kg (2 lb) fresh rice noodles, sliced
  into 2 cm (3/4 inch) strips
100 g (3 1/2 oz) garlic chives, chopped
2 1/2 tablespoons oyster sauce, extra
3 teaspoons soy sauce, extra
1 teaspoon sugar

1 Combine the garlic, ginger, oyster and soy sauces, add the beef and toss to coat. Cover and refrigerate for 30 minutes.
2 Heat the wok until very hot, add 1 tablespoon of the oil and swirl it around to coat the side. Add half the beef and stir-fry for 5 minutes, or until cooked. Remove and repeat with the remaining beef. Add another tablespoon of oil, then add the noodles and stir-fry for 3–5 minutes, or until softened.
3 Add the garlic chives and stir-fry until just wilted. Stir in the extra oyster and soy sauces and sugar, return the beef to the wok and toss to heat through. Serve immediately.

NUTRITION PER SERVE (6)
Protein 33 g; Fat 13 g; Carbohydrate 40 g;
Dietary Fibre 1.5 g; Cholesterol 50 mg;
1295 kJ (310 Cal)

Buy the fresh rice noodle as a block and cut it into thin strips.

Mix together the garlic, ginger, oyster and soy sauces to marinate the beef.

Stir-fry the noodles until they are softened, then add the garlic chives.

47

PHAD THAI

Preparation time: 35 minutes
Total cooking time: 10–15 minutes
Serves 4

250 g (8 oz) thick rice stick noodles
2 tablespoons oil
3 cloves garlic, chopped
2 teaspoons chopped red chillies
150 g (5 oz) pork, thinly sliced
100 g (3¹/₂ oz) peeled raw prawns, chopped
¹/₂ bunch garlic chives, chopped
2 tablespoons fish sauce
2 tablespoons lime juice
2 teaspoons soft brown sugar
2 eggs, beaten
1 cup (90 g/3 oz) bean sprouts
sprigs of fresh coriander
3 tablespoons chopped roasted peanuts
crisp-fried onion, soft brown sugar and chopped peanuts, to serve

1 Soak the rice stick noodles in warm water for 10 minutes or until they are soft. Drain and set aside. Heat the wok until very hot, then add the oil and swirl to coat the side. When the oil is very hot, add the garlic, chilli and pork and stir-fry for 2 minutes.
2 Add the prawns and stir-fry for 3 minutes. Add the garlic chives and drained noodles to the wok; cover and cook for another minute.
3 Add the fish sauce, lime juice, sugar and eggs to the wok. Toss well until heated through.
4 Serve immediately, sprinkled with the bean sprouts, sprigs of coriander and chopped peanuts. Traditionally served with crisp-fried onion, soft brown sugar and more chopped peanuts on the side.

NUTRITION PER SERVE
Protein 20 g; Fat 17 g; Carbohydrate 20 g;
Dietary Fibre 2 g; Cholesterol 145 mg;
1334 kJ (320 Cal)

After stir-frying the pork for 2 minutes, stir in the chopped prawns.

Use two wooden spoons or a pair of tongs to toss the stir-fry.

CHICKEN DOMBURI

Preparation time: 35 minutes
Total cooking time: 30 minutes
Serves 4

2 cups (440 g/14 oz) short-grain rice
2 tablespoons oil
2 small chicken breasts (about
    250 g/8 oz), cut into thin strips
2 onions, thinly sliced
1/3 cup (80 ml/2³/₄ fl oz) shoyu
2 tablespoons mirin
1 teaspoon dashi granules
5 eggs, lightly beaten
2 sheets nori
2 spring onions, sliced

1 Wash the rice in a colander under cold running water until the water runs clear. Transfer the rice to a heavy-based pan, add 2¹/₂ cups (600 ml/ 20 fl oz) water and bring to the boil over high heat. Cover the pan with a tight-fitting lid and reduce the heat to as low as possible (otherwise the rice in the bottom of the pan will burn) and cook for 15 minutes. Turn the heat to very high, for 15–20 seconds, remove the pan from the heat and set aside for 12 minutes, without lifting the lid or the steam will escape.
2 Heat the oil in a frying pan over high heat. Add the chicken and stir-fry until tender. Remove the chicken from the pan and set aside. Reheat the pan, add the onion and cook, stirring occasionally, for 3 minutes, or until beginning to soften. Add 1/3 cup (80 ml/2³/₄ fl oz) water, the shoyu, mirin and dashi granules. Stir to dissolve the dashi, and bring to the boil. Cook for 3 minutes, or until the onion is tender.
3 Return the chicken to the pan and pour in the egg, stirring gently to break up. Cover and simmer over very low heat for 2–3 minutes, or until the egg is just set. Remove the pan from the heat. To make the nori crisp, hold it over low heat, moving it back and forward for about 15 seconds, and then crumble it into small pieces.
4 Transfer the rice to a serving dish, carefully spoon over the chicken and egg mixture and sprinkle with the nori. Garnish with the spring onion.

NUTRITION PER SERVE
Protein 32 g; Fat 18 g; Carbohydrate 90 g; Dietary Fibre 3.6 g; Cholesterol 256 mg; 2737 kJ (654 cal)

NOTES: Domburi is an earthenware dish, and food served in the dish is also known as domburi.
The Japanese technique of cooking rice uses a 'burst' of heat before the standing time. A rice cooker can be used to cook the rice if preferred.

Wash the rice well in a colander under cold running water.

Cook the onion for about 3 minutes, or until it begins to soften.

Pour the egg into the pan and stir gently to break it up.

UDON NOODLES WITH GINGER PORK AND PICKLES

Preparation time: 30 minutes
  + 20 minutes marinating
Total cooking time: 25 minutes
Serves 4

10 cm (4 inch) piece fresh ginger,
  peeled
pinch of sugar
200 g (6¹/₂ oz) pork loin
500 g (1 lb) dried udon noodles
2 tablespoons cornflour
2 tablespoons oil
150 g (5 oz) broccoli, cut into long
  thin florets
100 g (3¹/₂ oz) Chinese pickled
  vegetables, finely sliced

4 spring onions, sliced
3 tablespoons soy sauce
3 tablespoons mirin or sherry
1 Lebanese cucumber, halved and
  finely sliced
2 tablespoons toasted sesame seeds

1 Slice one third of the ginger paper-thin and place in a bowl, then finely grate the rest. Squeeze the grated ginger over the ginger slices and discard the dry pulp. Season well with salt, pepper and the sugar.
2 Cut the pork into 5 cm (2 inch) strips. Add to the ginger. Mix well and leave to marinate for 20 minutes.
3 Cook the noodles in plenty of salted boiling water for 12 minutes, or until tender. Drain, rinse and set aside.
4 Remove the ginger from the pork. Scatter the cornflour over the pork and

mix well. Heat half the oil in a wok over medium-high heat. Quickly stir-fry the pork until golden, adding the ginger at the end. Remove and set aside.
5 Heat the remaining oil and stir-fry the broccoli, pickles and spring onion for 30 seconds. Add 1 tablespoon of water, then cover and steam for 30 seconds.
6 Add the noodles, soy sauce and mirin to the wok and toss well until heated through. Add the pork and ginger and toss well. Divide between bowls, garnish with cucumber and sesame seeds and serve at once.

NUTRITION PER SERVE
Protein 30 g; Fat 15 g; Carbohydrate 105 g;
Dietary Fibre 4 g; Cholesterol 25 mg;
2880 kJ (685 cal)

Buy the Chinese pickled vegetables from Asian food stores and slice them finely.

Slice a third of the ginger as thinly as you can, then grate the rest over it.

Add the noodles, soy sauce and mirin to the wok and toss well.

CHICKEN WITH SOY AND HOKKIEN NOODLES

Preparation time: 10 minutes
  + 10 minutes standing
Total cooking time: 10 minutes
Serves 4

450 g (14 oz) Hokkien noodles
1 tablespoon oil
500 g (1 lb) chicken thigh fillets, trimmed and sliced
2 cloves garlic, chopped
5 cm (2 inch) piece fresh ginger, julienned
4 spring onions, sliced on the diagonal
2 carrots, finely sliced on the diagonal
250 g (8 oz) broccoli, cut into small florets
2 tablespoons mirin
4 tablespoons soy sauce
1 teaspoon soft brown sugar
2 tablespoons toasted sesame seeds

1 Cover the noodles with boiling water and leave for 10 minutes, or until tender.

2 Heat a wok over high heat, add the oil and swirl to coat the side. Add the chicken in batches and stir-fry for 5 minutes. Return all the chicken to the wok, add the garlic and ginger and cook for 1 minute, or until fragrant. Add the spring onion, carrot and broccoli and cook for 4–5 minutes, or until tender.

3 Mix together the mirin, soy sauce and sugar and stir into the chicken mixture. Drain the noodles, add to the wok and cook until heated through. Serve sprinkled with the sesame seeds.

NUTRITION PER SERVE
Protein 64 g; Fat 25 g; Carbohydrate 114 g; Dietary Fibre 12 g; Cholesterol 100 mg; 3930 kJ (939 cal)

Add the garlic and ginger to the chicken and stir-fry for a further minute.

Add the spring onion, carrot and broccoli to the wok and cook until tender.

Drain the noodles, add to the wok and cook until heated through.

FRIED CRISPY NOODLES (MEE GROB)

Preparation time: 30 minutes
Total cooking time: 20 minutes
Serves 4

100 g (3¹/₂ oz) rice vermicelli
2 cups (500ml/16 fl oz) oil, for deep-frying
100 g (3¹/₂ oz) fried bean curd, cut into matchsticks
2 cloves garlic, finely chopped
4 cm (1¹/₂ inch) piece ginger, grated
150 g (5 oz) chicken mince
100 g (3¹/₂ oz) raw prawn meat, finely chopped
1 tablespoon white vinegar
2 tablespoons fish sauce
2 tablespoons soft brown sugar
2 tablespoons chilli sauce
1 teaspoon chopped red chilli
2 small knobs pickled garlic, chopped
¹/₄ bunch fresh garlic chives, chopped
1 cup (30 g/1 oz) fresh coriander leaves

1 Place the vermicelli in a bowl of hot water for 1 minute. Drain and allow to dry for 20 minutes. Heat the oil in a wok or deep pan, add the bean curd in two batches and cook for 1 minute, or until golden and crisp. Drain.
2 Add the completely dry vermicelli to the wok in several batches and cook for 10 seconds, or until puffed and crisp. Remove from the oil immediately to prevent the vermicelli absorbing too much oil. Drain on paper towels and allow to cool.
3 Drain all but 1 tablespoon of the oil from the wok. Reheat wok over high heat and add the garlic, ginger, mince and prawn meat; stir-fry for 2 minutes or until golden brown. Add the vinegar, fish sauce, brown sugar, chilli sauce and chilli, and stir until boiling.
4 Just before serving, add the noodles and bean curd to the wok and toss thoroughly. Quickly toss through the pickled garlic, chives and coriander. Serve immediately.

NUTRITION PER SERVE
Protein 18 g; Fat 123 g; Carbohydrate 28 g;
Dietary Fibre 3 g; Cholesterol 56 mg;
5183 kJ (1238 cal)

Cook the bean curd for 1 minute until golden brown. Remove with wire mesh strainer.

Add the vermicelli to the wok in batches and cook until puffed and crisp.

Add the chopped garlic, grated ginger, mince and prawn meat to the wok.

Just before serving, return the noodles and bean curd to the wok, and toss.

CARAMEL PORK WITH SHANGHAI NOODLES

Preparation time: 15 minutes
Total cooking time: 2 hours 30 minutes
Serves 4

500 g (1 lb) Shanghai noodles
700 g (1 lb 5 oz) boneless pork belly
2 teaspoons peanut oil
150 g (5 oz) caster sugar
5 cloves garlic, crushed
5 slices fresh ginger, 5 mm (1/4 inch) thick
2 stems lemon grass (white part only), bruised
1 teaspoon ground white pepper
2 cups (500 ml/16 fl oz) chicken stock
31/2 tablespoons fish sauce
100 g (31/2 oz) canned bamboo shoots, well drained
4 spring onions, cut into 3 cm (11/4 inch) pieces
1 tablespoon lime juice
1 tablespoon chopped fresh coriander leaves (optional)

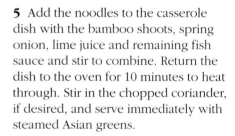

1 Cook the Shanghai noodles in a large saucepan of boiling water for 4–5 minutes, or until tender. Rinse, drain and cut into 10 cm lengths.
2 Preheat the oven to moderate 180°C (350°F/Gas 4). Cut the pork belly across the grain into 1 cm thick slices then cut each slice into 2 cm (3/4 inch) pieces. Heat the oil in a 4 litre clay pot or flameproof casserole dish over medium–high heat. Cook the pork in two batches for about 5 minutes, or until it starts to brown all over. Remove the pork and drain the fat.
3 Add the sugar and 2 tablespoons water to the casserole dish, stirring until the sugar has dissolved and scraping up any sediment that may

have stuck to the bottom. Increase the heat to high and cook for 2–3 minutes without stirring until dark golden, being careful not to burn—you should just be able to smell the caramel.
4 Return the pork to the casserole dish, then add the garlic, ginger, lemon grass, white pepper, stock, 2 tablespoons of the fish sauce and 11/2 cups (375 ml/12 fl oz) water and stir to combine. Bake, covered, for 1 hour then remove the lid and cook for another hour, or until the pork is very tender. Carefully remove the ginger slices and the lemon grass.

5 Add the noodles to the casserole dish with the bamboo shoots, spring onion, lime juice and remaining fish sauce and stir to combine. Return the dish to the oven for 10 minutes to heat through. Stir in the chopped coriander, if desired, and serve immediately with steamed Asian greens.

NUTRITION PER SERVE
Protein 48.5 g; Fat 7.5 g; Carbohydrate 73 g; Dietary Fibre 4 g; Cholesterol 166 mg; 2305 kJ (550 Cal)

Cut the pork belly across the grain into 1 cm thick slices.

Return the browned pork pieces to the caremel in the hotpot.

Remove the ginger slices and lemon grass from the hotpot.

CHICKEN AND CHILLI JAM NOODLES

Preparation time: 15 minutes +
  20 minutes soaking
Total cooking time: 10 minutes
Serves 4

250 g (8 oz) flat rice stick noodles
    (1 cm/^{1}/$_2$ inch wide)
400 g (13 oz) chicken breast fillet
1 onion
1 red capsicum
1 tablespoon peanut oil
2 tablespoons chilli jam (see Note)
2 teaspoons fish sauce
2 tablespoons light soy sauce
90 g (3 oz) bean sprouts
90 g (3 oz) unsalted cashew nuts
1 cup (30 g/1 oz) loosely packed fresh
    basil
2 tablespoons fresh basil, extra,
    to garnish

1 Place the noodles in a large heatproof bowl, cover with warm water and soak for 15–20 minutes. Drain well.
2 Cut the chicken breast fillets into 5 mm (^{1}/$_4$ inch) slices against the grain. Halve the onion and cut into thin wedges. Cut the capsicum in half, remove the seeds and membrane, then cut into thin strips with a sharp knife.
3 Heat a wok over high heat, add the peanut oil and swirl to coat the side. Cook the onion for 1–2 minutes, or until lightly golden. Add the chicken slices and cook for a further 3–5 minutes, or until browned and almost cooked through. Stir in the chilli jam, then add the capsicum and cook for another minute.
4 Add the fish sauce, soy sauce, bean sprouts, cashew nuts, basil and the noodles to the wok and toss until warmed through and well combined. Garnish with the extra basil and serve immediately.

NUTRITION PER SERVE
Protein 30.5 g; Fat 23 g; Carbohydrate 35 g; Dietary Fibre 4 g; Cholesterol 66 mg; 1960 kJ (470 Cal)

COOK'S FILE
Note: Chilli jam is made with tomato, onion, chilli, oil, tamarind, garlic, sugar, salt, spices and vinegar. It is available in Asian food stores.

SPICY NOODLES WITH PORK AND TOFU

Preparation time: 20 minutes
Total cooking time: 15 minutes
Serves 4

250 g (8 oz) Hokkien noodles
1 tablespoon oil
500 g (1 lb) pork fillet, thinly sliced
2 cloves garlic, crushed
2 cm x 2 cm (³/4 inch x ³/4 inch) piece
    fresh ginger, julienned
100 g (3¹/2 oz) snow peas, sliced
100 g (3¹/2 oz) fresh shiitake
    mushrooms, sliced
¹/2 teaspoon five-spice powder

2 tablespoons hoisin sauce
2 tablespoons soy sauce
¹/4 cup (60 ml/2 fl oz) vegetable stock
200 g (6¹/2 oz) fried tofu, sliced
100 g (3¹/2 oz) soy bean sprouts
fried red Asian shallot flakes,
    to garnish

1 Cook the noodles in a large saucepan of boiling water for 2–3 minutes, or until tender. Drain.
2 Heat a wok over high heat, add half the oil and swirl to coat. Add the pork in two batches and stir-fry for 2 minutes each batch, or until browned. Remove from the wok.
3 Add a little more oil if necessary, then add the garlic and ginger and stir-fry for 30 seconds, or until fragrant. Add the snow peas, mushrooms and five-spice powder and cook for a further 1 minute. Pour in the hoisin sauce, soy sauce and stock and cook, stirring constantly, for 1–2 minutes. Add the tofu, soy bean sprouts, noodles and pork and toss to warm through.
4 Serve immediately, garnished with the fried shallot flakes.

NUTRITION PER SERVE
Protein 45 g; Fat 16 g; Carbohydrate 55 g;
Dietary Fibre 9.5 g; Cholesterol 75 mg;
2293 kJ (548 Cal)

Use a sharp knife to slice the pork fillets into thin slices.

Stir-fry the pork slices in batches until browned all over.

Add the hoisin and soy sauces and stock and cook for a further 1–2 minutes.

RICE STICKS STIR-FRIED WITH CHICKEN AND GREENS

Preparation time: 25 minutes
Total cooking time: 10 minutes
Serves 4

6 baby bok choy
8 stems Chinese broccoli
150 g (5 oz) dried rice stick noodles
2 tablespoons oil
375 g (12 oz) chicken breast fillets
    or tenderloins, cut into
    thin strips
2–3 cloves garlic, crushed
5 cm (2 inch) piece ginger, grated
6 spring onions, cut into short pieces
1 tablespoon sherry
1 cup (90 g/3 oz) bean sprouts

SAUCE
2 teaspoons cornflour
2 tablespoons soy sauce
2 tablespoons oyster sauce
2 teaspoons soft brown sugar
1 teaspoon sesame oil

1 Remove any tough outer leaves from the bok choy and Chinese broccoli. Cut into 4 cm (1 1/2 inch) pieces across the leaves, including the stems. Wash well, then drain and dry thoroughly.
2 Place the rice stick noodles in a large heatproof bowl and cover with boiling water. Soak for 5–8 minutes, or until softened. Rinse, then drain. Cut into short lengths using scissors.
3 Meanwhile, to make the sauce, combine the cornflour and soy sauce in a small bowl. Mix to a smooth paste, then stir in the oyster sauce, brown sugar, sesame oil and 1/2 cup (125 ml/ 4 fl oz) water.
4 Heat a wok until very hot, add the oil and swirl it around to coat the side. Stir-fry the chicken strips, garlic, ginger and spring onion in batches over high heat for 3–4 minutes, or until the chicken is cooked. Remove from the wok and set aside.
5 Add the chopped bok choy, Chinese broccoli and sherry to the wok, cover and steam for 2 minutes, or until the vegetables are wilted. Remove from the wok and set aside.

Cut the bok choy and Chinese broccoli into pieces, including the stems.

Using a pair of scissors, cut the soaked noodles into short lengths.

Add the sauce to the wok and stir until the sauce is glossy and slightly thickened. Return the chicken, vegetables, noodles and bean sprouts to the wok, and stir until well combined and heated through. Serve at once.

NUTRITION PER SERVE
Protein 30 g; Fat 15 g; Carbohydrate 50 g; Dietary Fibre 4 g; Cholesterol 45 mg; 1855 kJ (445 cal)

NOTE: Broccoli and English spinach may be used as the greens.

TOFU AND PEANUT NOODLES

Preparation time: 10 minutes
Total cooking time: 10 minutes
Serves 4

250 g (8 oz) firm tofu, cut into small
    pieces
2 cloves garlic, crushed
1 teaspoon grated fresh ginger
1/3 cup (80 ml/2³/4 fl oz) kecap manis
1/3 cup (90 g/3 oz) peanut butter
2 tablespoons peanut or vegetable oil
500 g (1 lb) Hokkien noodles
1 onion, chopped

1 red capsicum, chopped
125 g (4 oz) broccoli, cut into small
    florets

1 Combine the tofu with the garlic, ginger and half the kecap manis in a small bowl. Place the peanut butter, 1/2 cup (125 ml/4 fl oz) water and the remaining kecap manis in another bowl and mix well.

2 Heat the oil in a large wok. Drain the tofu and reserve the marinade. Cook the tofu in two batches in the hot oil until well browned. Remove from the wok.

3 Place the noodles in a large heatproof bowl. Cover with boiling water and leave for 2 minutes. Drain and gently pull the noodles apart.

4 Add the vegetables to the wok and stir-fry until just tender. Add the tofu, reserved marinade and noodles. Add the peanut butter mixture and toss until heated through.

NUTRITION PER SERVE
Protein 32 g; Fat 30 g; Carbohydrate 96 g; Dietary Fibre 8 g; Cholesterol 20 mg; 3140 kJ (697 cal)

NOTE: Kecap manis is an Indonesian sweet soy sauce. If you are unable to find it, use soy sauce sweetened with a little soft brown sugar.

Mix together the tofu, garlic, ginger and half the kecap manis in a bowl.

Cook the tofu in two batches in the hot oil until it is well browned.

Soak the noodles in boiling water for a couple of minutes and then gently pull them apart.

HAINAN CHICKEN RICE

Preparation time: 30 minutes
Total cooking time: 1 hour 30 minutes
Serves 4

1.5 kg (3 lb) chicken
1 sprig celery leaves
2 spring onions, roughly chopped
1 teaspoon salt
peppercorns
1/4 cup (60 ml/2 fl oz) peanut oil
1 tablespoon sesame oil
1 tablespoon finely grated fresh ginger
2 teaspoons finely grated garlic
1 large onion, thinly sliced
2 cups (440 g/14 oz) short-grain rice
1/2 cup (25 g/3/4 oz) finely shredded
    Chinese cabbage
2 tablespoons chopped fresh
    coriander

DIPPING SAUCES
1 tablespoon finely grated fresh ginger
2 tablespoons soy sauce
1 red chilli, chopped

1 Place the chicken in a large pan with the celery leaves, spring onion, salt and a few peppercorns. Cover with water. Bring to the boil, covered, reduce the heat and simmer for 15 minutes. Turn off the heat and leave, covered, for 45 minutes.
2 Heat the oils in a pan with a tight-fitting lid. Add the ginger, garlic and onion and cook until soft and golden. Set aside 1 tablespoon of the oil.
3 Add the rice and cook, stirring, for 2 minutes. Add 3 cups (750 ml/24 fl oz) of the chicken cooking liquid. Bring to the boil, then reduce the heat and simmer until holes appear in the rice. Cover the pan tightly and reduce the

heat to very low. Cook for 15 minutes. Remove the lid, and fluff up the rice with a fork.
4 While the rice is cooking, remove the chicken from the pan, retaining the stock. Cut the chicken into pieces, arrange on a platter and keep warm.
5 To make the dipping sauces, combine the reserved cooking oils with the ginger. For the second sauce, combine the soy sauce with the chilli.
6 Strain the remaining chicken cooking liquid into a pan. Bring to the boil, then add the Chinese cabbage. Pour the soup into a bowl and sprinkle with the coriander. Serve the chicken, rice and dipping sauces with the soup.

NUTRITION PER SERVE
Protein 65 g; Fat 25 g; Carbohydrate 84 g;
Dietary Fibre 4 g; Cholesterol 125 mg;
3465 kJ (828 cal)

Cook the ginger, garlic and onion in the oils until soft and golden.

Simmer the rice and stock mixture until holes appear in the rice.

Use poultry scissors to cut the chicken into pieces for serving.

FRIED KOREAN NOODLES WITH PRAWNS

Preparation time: 30 minutes
Total cooking time: 25 minutes
Serves 4

3 tablespoons sesame seeds
2 tablespoons oil
2 teaspoons sesame oil
4 spring onions, chopped
2 cloves garlic, finely chopped
150 g (5 oz) peeled raw prawns
2 teaspoons finely chopped red chillies
150 g (5 oz) firm tofu, diced

100 g (3¹/₂ oz) button mushrooms, thinly sliced
1 red capsicum, cut into thin strips
2 tablespoons shoshoyu
2 teaspoons sugar
300 g (10 oz) packet Hokkien noodles

1 Dry-fry the sesame seeds over low heat for 3–4 minutes until golden. Cool and then grind in a mortar and pestle.
2 Combine the oils. Heat half the oil in the wok over medium-high heat. Stir-fry the spring onion, garlic and prawn meat for 1 minute. Add the chilli and cook for another minute. Remove from the wok.
3 Add the tofu to the wok and stir-fry until lightly golden, then remove. Add the remaining oil to the wok, add the mushrooms and capsicum and stir-fry for 3 minutes or until just crisp.
4 Add the shoshoyu, sugar, noodles and 2 tablespoons water to the wok. Toss gently to separate and coat the noodles in liquid. Cover and steam for 5 minutes. Add the prawn mixture and tofu and toss for 3 minutes over medium heat. Sprinkle with the crushed sesame seeds and serve.

NUTRITION PER SERVE
Protein 20 g; Fat 25 g; Carbohydrate 55 g;
Dietary Fibre 5 g; Cholesterol 70 mg;
2020 kJ (480 cal)

Stir-fry the onion, garlic and prawn meat for a minute and then add the chilli.

Stir-fry the tofu, tossing occasionally, until lightly golden. Remove and set aside.

Add the shoshoyu, sugar, noodles and water to the wok and toss gently.

JASMINE RICE WITH PRAWNS

Preparation time: 15 minutes
Total cooking time: 30 minutes
Serves 4

1 tablespoon peanut oil
8 spring onions, sliced
1 tablespoon finely chopped fresh
    ginger
1 tablespoon finely sliced lemon grass,
    white part only
2 teaspoons crushed coriander seeds
    (see NOTE)
2 cups (400 g/13 oz) jasmine rice
4 cups (1 litre) vegetable stock
1 tablespoon shredded lime rind
1 kg (2 lb) raw prawns, peeled,
    deveined and chopped
2 tablespoons lime juice
1 cup (30 g/1 oz) fresh coriander
    leaves
fish sauce, for serving

1 Heat the oil in a saucepan, add the spring onion and cook over low heat for 4 minutes, or until soft. Add the ginger, lemon grass, coriander seeds and rice, and stir for 1 minute.
2 Add the stock and lime rind and bring to the boil while stirring. Reduce the heat to very low and cook, covered, for 15–20 minutes, or until the rice is tender.
3 Remove the pan from the heat and stir in the prawns. Cover and leave for 4–5 minutes, or until the prawns are cooked. Add the lime juice and coriander leaves and flake the rice with a fork. Sprinkle with a few drops of fish sauce to serve.

NUTRITION PER SERVE
Protein 59 g; Fat 12 g; Carbohydrate 80 g;
Dietary Fibre 3 g; Cholesterol 373 mg;
2850 kJ (681 cal)

NOTE: To crush coriander seeds, place in a small plastic bag and, using a rolling pin, crush until fine.

Peel and devein the prawns and chop them into small pieces.

Add the ginger, lemon grass, coriander seeds and rice to the saucepan.

Add the lime juice and coriander leaves and flake the rice with a fork.

SWEET AND SOUR NOODLES

Preparation time: 12 minutes
Total cooking time: 15 minutes
Serves 4–6

200 g (6½ oz) thin fresh egg noodles
3 tablespoons oil
1 green capsicum, sliced
1 red capsicum, sliced
2 sticks celery, sliced diagonally
1 carrot, sliced diagonally
250 g (8 oz) button mushrooms, sliced
4 fresh baby corn spears, sliced on
    the diagonal
3 teaspoons cornflour

2 tablespoons brown vinegar
1 teaspoon chopped fresh chilli
2 teaspoons tomato paste
2 chicken stock cubes, crumbled
1 teaspoon sesame oil
450 g (14 oz) can chopped pineapple
    pieces
3 spring onions, sliced diagonally

1 Cook the noodles in boiling water for 3 minutes; drain well. Heat the oil in a wok and stir-fry the capsicum, celery, carrot and mushrooms over high heat for 5 minutes.
2 Add the corn and noodles to the wok. Reduce the heat to low and cook for 2 minutes.
3 Blend the cornflour and vinegar into

a smooth paste. Add the chilli, tomato paste, stock cubes, oil and undrained pineapple to the paste and stir well.
4 Pour the pineapple mixture into the wok. Stir over medium heat for 5 minutes or until the sauce has boiled and thickened. Add the spring onions and serve immediately.

NUTRITION PER SERVE (6)
Protein 8 g; Fat 12 g; Carbohydrate 36 g;
Dietary Fibre 5 g; Cholesterol 6 mg;
1182 kJ (282 cal)

VARIATION: Thinly sliced Chinese barbecued pork (*char siew*) can be added to this stir-fry.

Slice the celery, carrot and baby corn on the diagonal for an attractive stir-fry.

Cook the capsicum, celery, carrot and mushrooms, before adding the corn and noodles.

Stir in the spring onions just before serving, once the sauce has thickened.

CHINESE NOODLES WITH PRAWNS AND PORK

Preparation time: 20 minutes
Total cooking time: 10 minutes
Serves 4

500 g (1 lb) Hokkien noodles,
    gently pulled apart
3 tablespoons peanut oil
2 teaspoons finely chopped garlic
10 large cooked prawns,
    peeled and deveined
200 g (6¹/₂ oz) roast or Chinese
    barbecued pork, thinly sliced
1 tablespoon black bean sauce
1 tablespoon soy sauce
1 tablespoon chilli and ginger sauce
1 tablespoon white vinegar
3 tablespoons chicken stock
125 g (4 oz) bean sprouts,
    tails removed
3 spring onions, finely sliced
¹/₄ cup (15 g/¹/₂ oz) chopped
    coriander

1 Cover the noodles with boiling water and stir with a fork to separate them. Leave for a couple of minutes to soften, then drain.
2 Heat a wok, add the oil and place over medium heat, swirling gently to coat the base and side of the wok with oil. Add the garlic and stir-fry until pale gold. Add the prawns and pork and stir-fry for 1 minute.
3 Add the noodles to the wok with the sauces, vinegar and stock. Stir-fry over high heat until the mixture has heated through and the sauce has been absorbed into the noodles.
4 Add the bean sprouts and the spring onion and cook for 1 minute. Serve immediately, sprinkled with coriander.

NUTRITION PER SERVE
Protein 26 g; Fat 18 g; Carbohydrate 30 g;
Dietary Fibre 2 g; Cholesterol 82 mg;
1600 kJ (382 cal)

VARIATION: Fresh, thick, egg and wheat noodles (hokkien mee) are ideal for Chinese stir-fries. They require just a couple of minutes in boiling water to soften them before use. If Hokkien noodles are unavailable, you can use thick spaghetti, cooked first in plenty of boiling water until tender.

NOTE: Chinese barbecued pork can be bought from Chinese supermarkets and groceries.

The noodles need just a couple of minutes in hot water to soften them.

Stir-fry the garlic, then add the pork and prawns and cook for 1 minute.

Add the bean sprouts and spring onion to the wok and cook for 1 minute.

stir-fries

Stir-fry Know-how

Once the ingredients are prepared, the secret of stir-frying is to cook quickly over high heat and keep the food moving constantly around the wok.

Stir-frying is a fast, relatively healthy way to cook food. It involves quick cooking where the food is tossed around in a wok over high heat in a minimum amount of oil (although we have also included some recipes that combine initial stir-frying of ingredients with a short simmer to produce typical Asian curries). Preparation of ingredients is essential because once you start to cook there is no time to chop anything extra or hunt through cupboards.

OILS

For stir-frying, use oils that have a high smoking point. These include canola oil and peanut oil. Olive oil may be used to add flavour to warm stir-fry salads. If you are trying to cut down on fat, use an oil spray.

INGREDIENTS

Meat and Poultry: Meat to be stir-fried needs to be from a cut which will be tender after only a short cooking time. It should be cut across the grain into strips or small pieces so that it cooks quickly and evenly. Use chicken breast or thigh. Marinating meat or chicken helps to tenderize it and allows flavours to permeate the meat. Make sure the marinade is drained well before stir-frying, otherwise the meat or chicken will tend to steam rather than fry.
Seafood: Quick cooking suits seafood perfectly. Squid, prawns and scallops need the briefest possible time in the wok until they are cooked through. Use firm-fleshed fish so it can be stir-fried without breaking up.
Vegetables: Stir-frying affects different vegetables in different ways. The intense heat caramelizes their sugar, but retains most of their vitamins and colour. Vegetables such as cauliflower,

potatoes and carrots require a slightly longer cooking time and should be cut into small pieces or thin strips, whereas peas, asparagus and mushrooms should be cooked quickly at the end. Bean sprouts, herbs and greens, such as bok choy and spinach, should be added for the final minute or so, but for no longer because they will wilt quickly.

WOKS

There are many different types of wok available. The traditional basic wok is made of carbon steel. In its modern form the wok comes made of copper, stainless steel, cast iron and non-stick materials. Buy the heaviest wok you can find as it will retain heat well without scorching. You can also buy electric woks—these are non-stick and are kept at a constant high heat by an electric element.

The shape of a wok should be wide with deep, sloping sides and a round or wide, flattish bottom. It should be about 30–35 cm (12–14 inches) in diameter as small amounts of food can be cooked easily enough in a large wok but not vice versa. Flat-bottomed woks work well on electric stovetops as they sit directly on the hotplate—a wok ring often holds the wok too far away from the heat source for successful stir-frying. Some of the more modern stovetops have a special wide gas burner for woks.

Wok lids are important as they can be used to form a seal for a couple of minutes to steam any slower cooking ingredients or greens. Many recipes will instruct you to cover the wok for a short time at the end of cooking.

If you do not have a wok, you can use a large heavy-based frying pan for stir-frying, but you will need to cook the food in smaller batches to prevent it stewing.

SEASONING THE WOK

Steel woks come with an oily film which needs to be scrubbed off with hot water and detergent before use. The wok should then be dried off and heated over high heat. When it starts to become hot, brush it with vegetable oil, remove it from the heat and wipe it dry with a paper towel (it will blacken

You can buy electric woks that are non-stick and are kept at a constant high heat by an element.

The oily film on a new wok has to be scrubbed off before use.

A wok will blacken as you season it and turn darker as you use it.

as you season it). Repeat this step several times to season the wok. As you use the wok, the seasoned layer (*wok hay*) will build up, turning darker and darker and adding flavour to the food.

A properly seasoned or a non-stick wok shouldn't be cleaned by scouring with an abrasive material like steel wool. Each time, after you have finished cooking and your wok has cooled down, simply wash it with hot water and a soft brush or cloth. Make sure you dry it throroughly over heat before storing in a dry area, otherwise it will rust. If you have a steel wok you should wipe or brush the inside with a very thin layer of oil before putting it away. This will keep it in good condition. Electric woks should also be rinsed in hot water, dried very thoroughly and coated with a thin film of oil after use.

The outside of the wok may occasionally need a good clean. Try not to used detergents—they damage the seasoning. If you do burn a stir-fry, you may need to use detergent and even a fine steel wool to clean the wok and may need to re-season.

WOK TOOLS

Utensils needed to stir-fry are minimal—a sharp knife for preparation and a wok turner or *charn*. This is a spade-like scoop, ideal for the continuous scooping and turning required. Flat spatulas also work well because they move the food around easily and follow the curvature of the wok.

Only wooden or plastic utensils should be used on non-stick woks so that the surface is not scratched.

Mesh ladles, a charn and chopsticks—ideal tools for cooking and eating stir-fries.

TEN STEPS FOR SUCCESSFUL STIR-FRYING

1 The most important thing is to have everything ready before you start to stir-fry. Arrange all the ingredients in bowls in the order you are going to cook them and measure out any liquids, pastes, sauces or cornflour that you might be adding. Once you start cooking, it is hard to stop and chop something up without overcooking whatever is already in the wok.

2 Cut all meat and vegetables into even-sized, smallish pieces. The smaller the pieces, the faster they will cook.

3 Choose vegetables which will look colourful as well as taste good with the other ingredients.

4 Heat the wok until very hot before you add the oil. When you add the oil, swirl it around to thoroughly coat the side and base of the wok. Do not start cooking until the oil is hot—the oil will start to shimmer when it is hot enough and will hiss when the first ingredients go in.

5 Drain any marinade from the ingredients before cooking and make sure all vegetables are quite dry. If any liquid hits the hot oil first, it will spit. If meat is added to the wok straight from a wet marinade, the meat will tend to steam or stew rather than fry.

6 Add the flavourings, such as ginger and garlic, first, then add the slower-cooking ingredients, followed by the faster-cooking ones. If you have too much to fit in the wok at one time, fry the meat first in batches and set it aside, otherwise it will stew. Reheat the wok between batches, adding a little more oil if necessary. Salty liquids, such as soy sauce, should be added at the end as they may draw water out of the vegetables and make them mushy.

7 Keep all the ingredients moving constantly around the wok to make sure everything cooks evenly and doesn't start to burn.

8 If an ingredient looks as if it might burn, quickly add the next ingredient to reduce the temperature of the wok.

9 If the ingredients start to look a little dry, add a splash of water.

10 Serve immediately—stir-fries don't wait for anyone!

Heat the wok, add the oil and swirl it around to coat the base and side of the wok.

When the oil starts to shimmer, add the first ingredients and toss well.

Stir-fry meat in batches if there is a lot of it, to prevent it stewing.

Keep the food moving to ensure even cooking and prevent burning.

BEEF WITH LEEKS AND SNOW PEAS

Preparation time: 25 minutes
Total cooking time: 15 minutes
Serves 4

oil, for cooking
375 g (12 oz) rump steak, cut into very
    thin strips
2–3 cloves garlic, finely chopped
1 stem lemon grass, white part only,
    finely chopped
1 leek, white part only, thinly sliced
2 celery sticks, thickly sliced
8 spring onions, diagonally sliced
150 g (5 oz) snow peas, halved
100 g (3½ oz) oyster mushrooms,
    halved
2 tablespoons kecap manis
2 tablespoons sweet chilli sauce
2 tablespoons lime or lemon juice
3 kaffir lime leaves, shredded (see
    HINT)
1 tablespoon fish sauce

1 Heat the wok until very hot, add
1 tablespoon of the oil and swirl it
around to coat the side. Stir-fry the
beef strips, garlic and lemon grass in
two or three batches over high heat for
2–3 minutes, or until the beef is browned. Remove all the beef mixture
from the wok.

2 Reheat the wok, add 1 tablespoon
of the oil and stir-fry the leek, celery
and spring onion for 2 minutes. Add
the snow peas and oyster mushrooms,
and stir-fry for 1–2 minutes, or until
tender. Remove the vegetables from
the wok and set aside.

3 Add the combined kecap manis,
chilli sauce and lime or lemon juice to
the wok, and bring to the boil. Return
all the beef and vegetables to the wok
and stir-fry for 1–2 minutes, or until
the beef has just heated through and
everything is well coated with the
sauce. Toss the shredded kaffir lime
leaves through the mixture and
sprinkle with the fish sauce, to taste.
Serve at once.

NUTRITION PER SERVE
Protein 25 g; Fat 13 g; Carbohydrate 8.5 g;
Dietary Fibre 5 g; Cholesterol 65 mg;
1065 kJ (255 cal)

HINT: If kaffir lime leaves are not
available, sprinkle the stir-fry with
3 tablespoons chopped fresh basil
leaves just before serving. (If you
chop and add them earlier they tend
to turn black.)

Finely chop the white part of the lemon grass
stem, discarding the green part.

Stir-fry the beef, garlic and lemon grass until the
beef browns.

HONEY CHICKEN

Preparation time: 15 minutes
Total cooking time: 25 minutes
Serves 4

oil, for cooking
500 g (1 lb) chicken thigh fillets,
    cut into cubes
1 egg white, lightly beaten
1/3 cup (40 g/1 1/4 oz) cornflour
2 onions, thinly sliced
1 green capsicum, cubed
2 carrots, cut into batons
100 g (3 1/2 oz) snow peas,
    sliced

1/4 cup (90 g/3 oz) honey
2 tablespoons toasted almonds

1 Heat a wok until very hot, add
1 1/2 tablespoons of the oil and swirl it
around to coat the side. Dip half of the
chicken into the egg white, then lightly
dust with the cornflour. Stir-fry over
high heat for 4–5 minutes, or until the
chicken is golden brown and just
cooked. Remove from the wok and
drain on paper towels. Repeat with
the remaining chicken, then remove
all the chicken from the wok.
2 Reheat the wok, add 1 tablespoon
of the oil and stir-fry the sliced onion
over high heat for 3–4 minutes, or until

slightly softened. Add the capsicum
and carrot, and cook, tossing, for
3–4 minutes, or until tender. Stir in
the snow peas and cook for 2 minutes.
3 Increase the heat, add the honey
and toss the vegetables until well
coated. Return the chicken to the wok
and toss until it is heated through and
is well coated in the honey. Remove
from the heat and season well with
salt and pepper. Serve immediately,
sprinkled with the almonds.

NUTRITION PER SERVE
Protein 35 g; Fat 20 g; Carbohydrate 35 g;
Dietary Fibre 4 g; Cholesterol 60 mg;
1815 kJ (435 Cal)

Trim the excess fat from the chicken, and cut the
chicken into cubes.

Dip the chicken into the egg white, then lightly
dust with the cornflour.

Stir-fry the chicken pieces until golden brown and
just cooked.

BARBECUED PORK AND BROCCOLI

Preparation time: 25 minutes
Total cooking time: 10 minutes
Serves 4–6

1 tablespoon oil
1 large onion, thinly sliced
2 carrots, cut into matchsticks
200 g (6½ oz) broccoli, chopped
6 spring onions, diagonally sliced
1 tablespoon finely chopped fresh
    ginger

3 cloves garlic, finely chopped
400 g (13 oz) Chinese barbecued
    pork, thinly sliced
2 tablespoons soy sauce
2 tablespoons mirin
2 cups (180 g/6 oz) bean sprouts

1 Heat the wok until very hot, add the oil and swirl it around to coat the side. Stir-fry the onion over medium heat for 3–4 minutes, or until slightly softened. Add the carrot, broccoli, spring onion, ginger and garlic and cook for 4–5 minutes, tossing the mixture constantly.

2 Increase the heat to high and add the barbecued pork. Toss constantly until the pork is well mixed with the vegetables and is heated through. Add the soy sauce and mirin, and toss until the ingredients are well coated. (The wok should be hot enough for the sauce to reduce into a glaze.) Add the bean sprouts and season well with salt and pepper. Serve immediately.

NUTRITION PER SERVE (6)
Protein 20 g; Fat 15 g; Carbohydrate 6.5 g;
Dietary Fibre 6 g; Cholesterol 40 mg;
920 kJ (220 Cal)

Peel the carrots, if necessary, and cut them into even-sized matchsticks.

Cut the pieces of Chinese barbecued pork into thin slices.

Add the pork to the wok and toss until it is well mixed with the vegetables.

TOFU WITH SHOSHOYU AND MIRIN

Preparation time: 20 minutes
+ 2 hours marinating
Total cooking time: 20 minutes
Serves 4

500 g (1 lb) firm tofu (see HINT), cut into small cubes
1/3 cup (80 ml/2³/4 fl oz) shoshoyu (Japanese soy sauce)
1/4 cup (60 ml/2 fl oz) mirin
3 cloves garlic, finely chopped
2 tablespoons finely chopped fresh ginger
oil, for cooking
1 onion, thinly sliced
2 carrots, cut into batons
1 red capsicum, thinly sliced
150 g (5 oz) snow peas, thinly sliced

1 Combine the tofu with the shoshoyu, mirin, garlic and ginger in a glass or ceramic bowl. Cover and refrigerate for 2 hours.
2 Heat the wok until very hot, add 1 tablespoon of the oil and swirl it around to coat the side. Drain the tofu, reserving the marinade. Stir-fry the tofu in three batches over high heat until it is golden brown. Heat 1 tablespoon of the oil between batches. Remove all the tofu from the wok and drain on paper towels.
3 Reheat the wok, add 1 tablespoon of the oil and stir-fry the onion, carrot and capsicum over medium-high heat for 3–4 minutes, or until the vegetables are tender. Add the snow peas and cook for 3 minutes.
4 Increase the heat to high and add the reserved marinade, tossing the vegetables in the marinade until they are thoroughly coated and the sauce boils. Return the tofu to the wok and toss until the mixture is well combined and the tofu is heated through. Season well with salt and pepper, and serve immediately.

NUTRITION PER SERVE
Protein 15 g; Fat 15 g; Carbohydrate 9 g; Dietary Fibre 4 g; Cholesterol 0 mg; 930 kJ (220 cal)

HINT: Tofu does not have a strong flavour of its own but takes on flavour from whatever it is mixed with. Choose the firmest tofu you can find for this recipe. Tempeh could also be used.

Buy the firmest tofu you can find, drain it and cut into bite-sized cubes.

Combine the tofu, shoshoyu, mirin, garlic and ginger in a bowl and leave to marinate.

LEMON CHICKEN

Preparation time: 15 minutes
  + 30 minutes marinating
Total cooking time: 10 minutes
Serves 4

500 g (1 lb) chicken breast fillets
1 egg white, lightly beaten
2 teaspoons cornflour
1/2 teaspoon salt
1/4 teaspoon grated ginger
1/4 cup (60 ml/2 fl oz) oil

LEMON SAUCE
2 teaspoons cornflour
1 1/2 tablespoons caster sugar

2 tablespoons lemon juice
3/4 cup (185 ml/6 fl oz) chicken stock
2 teaspoons soy sauce
1 teaspoon dry sherry

1 Pat the chicken dry with paper towels. Cut the chicken fillets on the diagonal into 1 cm (1/2 inch) wide strips. Combine the egg white, cornflour, salt and ginger and add the chicken strips, mixing well. Marinate in the refrigerator for 30 minutes.
2 Heat the oil in a wok or heavy-based frying pan, swirling to coat. Drain the chicken from the marinade, add to the pan and stir-fry over medium-high heat until just cooked but not browned. Place the chicken on a plate to keep warm while preparing the sauce. Carefully pour the excess oil from the wok and discard.
3 To make the lemon sauce, mix the cornflour with 2 tablespoons water to form a smooth paste. Add to the wok with the sugar, lemon juice, chicken stock, soy sauce and sherry. Stir over high heat and boil for 1 minute. Add the chicken, stirring to coat it with the sauce. Transfer to a serving platter. Serve at once with steamed rice or noodles and stir-fried vegetables.

NUTRITION PER SERVE
Protein 29 g; Fat 17 g; Carbohydrate 8 g;
Dietary Fibre 0 g; Cholesterol 63 mg;
1280 kJ (306 cal)

Cut the chicken breast fillets on the diagonal into thin strips.

Stir-fry the marinated chicken until it is just cooked but not browned.

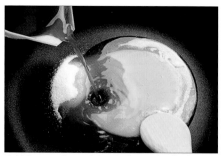

Add the cornflour mixture to the wok with the sugar, lemon juice, stock, soy sauce and sherry.

ASIAN GREENS WITH TERIYAKI TOFU DRESSING

Preparation time: 15 minutes
Total cooking time: 20 minutes
Serves 6

650 g (1 lb 5 oz) baby bok choy
500 g (1 lb) choy sum
440 g (14 oz) snake beans,
    topped and tailed
1/4 cup (60 ml/2 fl oz) oil
1 onion, thinly sliced
1/3 cup (60 g/2 oz) soft brown sugar
1/2 teaspoon ground chilli

2 tablespoons grated fresh ginger
1 cup (250 ml/8 fl oz) teriyaki sauce
1 tablespoon sesame oil
600 g (1 1/4 lb) silken firm tofu, drained

1 Cut the the baby bok choy and choy sum widthways into thirds. Chop the snake beans into shorter lengths.
2 Heat a wok over high heat, add 1 tablespoon of the oil and swirl to coat the side. Cook the onion for 3–5 minutes, or until crisp. Remove with a slotted spoon and drain on paper towels.
3 Heat 1 tablespoon of the oil in the wok, add half the greens and stir-fry for 2–3 minutes, or until wilted.

Remove and keep warm. Repeat with the remaining oil and greens. Remove. Drain any liquid from the wok.
4 Add the combined sugar, chilli, ginger and teriyaki sauce to the wok and bring to the boil. Simmer for 1 minute. Add the sesame oil and tofu and simmer for 2 minutes, turning once—the tofu will break up. Divide the greens among serving plates, then top with the dressing. Sprinkle with the fried onion to serve.

NUTRITION PER SERVE
Protein 19 g; Fat 11 g; Carbohydrate 20 g; Dietary Fibre 11 g; Cholesterol 1 mg; 1093 kJ (260 cal)

Cut the baby bok choy and choy sum widthways into thirds.

Cook the combined greens in two batches until the leaves are wilted.

Turn the tofu with an egg-flip halfway through the cooking time.

SWEET MUSTARD LAMB STIR-FRY

Preparation time: 15 minutes
Total cooking time: 15 minutes
Serves 4

oil, for cooking
500 g (1 lb) lamb fillet, cut into thin
   strips
2 cloves garlic, crushed
250 g (8 oz) snow peas
1 onion, cut into large wedges
20 g (³/₄ oz) butter
¹/₄ cup (60 g/2 oz) wholegrain mustard
1 tablespoon honey
¹/₂ cup (125 ml/4 fl oz) cream
2 tablespoons brandy, optional

1 Heat the wok until very hot, add
1 tablespoon of the oil and swirl it
around to coat the side. Stir-fry the
lamb strips in batches over high heat.
Remove from the wok and set aside.
2 Heat 1 tablespoon of the oil in the
wok and add the crushed garlic, snow
peas and onion wedges. Stir-fry over
medium heat for 3–4 minutes, or until
the onion softens slightly. Remove
from the wok and keep warm.
3 Reduce the heat and add the butter,
wholegrain mustard, honey, cream
and brandy to the wok. Simmer the
sauce gently for 3–4 minutes. Return
the meat and the snow pea mixture
to the wok and stir until the meat and
vegetables are heated through and
combined with the sauce.

NUTRITION PER SERVE
Protein 30 g; Fat 30 g; Carbohydrate 15 g;
Dietary Fibre 4 g; Cholesterol 140 mg;
2030 kJ (485 Cal)

Remove any fat or sinew from the lamb fillet and
cut the lamb into thin strips.

Stir-fry the lamb slices in batches over high heat
so that the meat browns.

Heat the oil and add the garlic, snow peas and
onion wedges.

SWORDFISH WITH BOK CHOY

Preparation time: 20 minutes
Total cooking time: 10 minutes
Serves 4

500 g (1 lb) swordfish steak, cubed
2 tablespoons cracked black pepper
oil, for cooking
3 cloves garlic, thinly sliced
1 onion, sliced
1 kg (2 lb) baby bok choy, leaves
    separated
100 g (3¹/₂ oz) shiitake mushrooms,
    sliced

2 tablespoons hoisin sauce
2 tablespoons rice wine
1 tablespoon oyster sauce
1 tablespoon soy sauce
1 tablespoon toasted sesame seeds
1 teaspoon sesame oil

1 Dip the swordfish in cracked black pepper until coated, then shake off any excess.
2 Heat the wok until very hot, add 2 tablespoons of the oil and swirl it around to coat the side. Stir-fry the swordfish in batches over high heat until tender. Do not overcook or the fish will break up. Remove from the wok and keep warm.

3 Reheat the wok, add 1 tablespoon of the oil and stir-fry the garlic until crisp and golden. Add the onion and stir-fry until golden. Add the bok choy and mushrooms and cook until the leaves wilt. Combine the hoisin sauce, rice wine, oyster sauce and soy sauce, pour into the wok and heat.
4 Return the swordfish to the wok and toss. Serve sprinkled with sesame seeds and drizzled with the oil.

NUTRITION PER SERVE
Protein 35 g; Fat 15 g; Carbohydrate 15 g;
Dietary Fibre 3 g; Cholesterol 90 mg;
1490 kJ (355 cal)

Use a sharp knife to cut the swordfish steak into bite-sized cubes.

Wipe the mushrooms with a damp paper towel, then cut into slices.

Dip the pieces of swordfish in the cracked black pepper and shake off any excess.

SICHUAN PORK WITH CAPSICUM

Preparation time: 30 minutes
Total cooking time: 10 minutes
Serves 4–6

1 1/2 tablespoons cornflour
1 tablespoon Sichuan peppercorns, ground
2 egg whites, beaten
500 g (1 lb) pork fillet, thinly sliced
2 tablespoons peanut oil, plus 1 teaspoon, extra
1 red capsicum, thinly sliced
2 spring onions, sliced into short lengths
2 teaspoons chilli oil
4 star anise
2 cloves garlic, crushed

2 teaspoons finely chopped fresh ginger
2 tablespoons oyster sauce
2 tablespoons Chinese rice wine
2 tablespoons soy sauce
1/2 teaspoon sesame oil
2 teaspoons sugar

1 Place the cornflour, peppercorns, egg whites and 1/2 teaspoon salt in a bowl. Mix well, then add the pork and toss to coat.

2 Heat a wok until very hot, add 1 teaspoon peanut oil and swirl to coat the base and side of the wok with oil. Add the capsicum and spring onion and stir-fry for 1 minute. Remove from the wok.

3 Add 1 tablespoon peanut oil to the wok and swirl to coat the base and side of the wok. Add half the pork and stir-fry for 2 minutes, or until sealed. Remove. Repeat with the remaining oil and pork.

4 Add the chilli oil to the wok and swirl to coat. Add the star anise and stir-fry for 30 seconds, then add the garlic and ginger and stir-fry for another few seconds.

5 Combine the oyster sauce, rice wine, soy sauce, sesame oil and sugar, add to the wok and cook for 30 seconds. Return the pork to the wok and stir-fry for 1 minute, then stir in the vegetables and serve.

NUTRITION PER SERVE (6)
Protein 20 g; Fat 11 g; Carbohydrate 4 g; Dietary Fibre 0.5 g; Cholesterol 40 mg; 865 kJ (207 cal)

Mix together the cornflour, peppercorns, egg whites and salt, then add the pork.

Stir-fry the capsicum and spring onion in the peanut oil for 1 minute.

Add half of the pork to the wok so that it doesn't overcrowd and stew in its juices.

CUCUMBER AND WHITE FISH STIR-FRY

Preparation time: 20 minutes
Total cooking time: 20 minutes
Serves 4

1/2 cup (60 g/2 oz) plain flour
1/2 cup (60 g/2 oz) cornflour
1/2 teaspoon Chinese five-spice
750 g (1 1/2 lb) firm white boneless fish fillets, such as ling, cut into cubes
2 egg whites, lightly beaten
oil, for deep-frying
1 tablespoon oil
1 onion, cut into wedges
1 telegraph cucumber, seeded, sliced

1 teaspoon cornflour, extra
3/4 teaspoon sesame oil
1 tablespoon soy sauce
1/3 cup (80 ml/2 3/4 fl oz) rice wine vinegar
1 1/2 tablespoons soft brown sugar
3 teaspoons fish sauce

1 Combine the flours and five-spice, and season with salt and pepper. Dip the fish in the egg white, drain off any excess, then toss in the flour. Shake off any excess.
2 Fill a large saucepan one-third full of oil and heat until a bread cube browns in 15 seconds. Cook the fish in batches for 6 minutes, or until golden brown. Drain and keep warm.

3 Heat a wok until very hot, add 1 tablespoon oil and swirl to coat. Add the onion and stir-fry for 1 minute. Add the cucumber and stir-fry for 30 seconds.
4 Blend the extra cornflour with 2 tablespoons water and add to the wok with the sesame oil, soy, vinegar, sugar and fish sauce. Stir-fry for 3 minutes, or until the mixture boils and thickens. Add the fish and toss to coat. Serve immediately.

NUTRITION PER SERVE
Protein 43 g; Fat 16 g; Carbohydrate 35 g;
Dietary Fibre 1 g; Cholesterol 130 mg;
1990 kJ (475 Cal)

Use boneless white fish fillets and cut them into bite-sized pieces.

Deep-fry the pieces of fish in oil, cooking in batches so the temperature stays high.

Stir-fry the mixture for 3 minutes, or until it boils and thickens, before adding the fish.

CHICKEN WITH WALNUTS AND STRAW MUSHROOMS

Preparation time: 20 minutes
Total cooking time: 15 minutes
Serves 4

375 g (12 oz) chicken breast fillets or
tenderloins, cut into thin strips
1/2 teaspoon five-spice powder
2 teaspoons cornflour
2 tablespoons soy sauce
2 tablespoons oyster sauce
2 teaspoons soft brown sugar
1 teaspoon sesame oil
oil, for cooking
75 g (2 1/2 oz) walnuts
150 g (5 oz) snake beans or green
beans, chopped

6 spring onions, sliced
425 g (14 oz) can straw mushrooms,
rinsed
230 g (7 1/2 oz) can sliced bamboo
shoots, rinsed

1 Dry the chicken strips with paper towels and sprinkle with the five-spice powder. Mix the cornflour with the soy sauce in a bowl until smooth. Add 1/2 cup (125 ml/4 fl oz) water along with the oyster sauce, brown sugar and sesame oil.

2 Heat the wok until very hot, add 1 tablespoon of the oil and swirl it around to coat the side. Stir-fry the walnuts for 30 seconds, or until lightly browned. Drain on paper towels.

3 Reheat the wok over high heat. Add 1 tablespoon of the oil and stir-fry the

chicken in batches for 2–3 minutes, or until just cooked through. Remove all of the chicken from the wok and set aside.

4 Add the snake beans, spring onion, straw mushrooms and bamboo shoots to the wok, and stir-fry for 2 minutes. Remove from the wok. Add the soy sauce mixture and heat for 1 minute, or until slightly thickened. Return the chicken and vegetables to the wok, and toss to coat with the sauce. Season well. Serve at once, sprinkled with the stir-fried walnuts.

NUTRITION PER SERVE
Protein 30 g; Fat 25 g; Carbohydrate 10 g;
Dietary Fibre 6.5 g; Cholesterol 45 mg;
1675 kJ (400 cal)

Wash the straw mushrooms in a sieve under cold running water.

Top and tail the snake beans, and cut them into short pieces.

Stir-fry the walnuts in the hot oil until they are lightly browned.

THAI BEEF SALAD

Preparation time: 20 minutes + cooling
Total cooking time: 5 minutes
Serves 6

oil, for cooking
500 g (1 lb) beef fillet or lean rump,
    thinly sliced
2 cloves garlic, crushed
1/4 cup (15 g/1/2 oz) finely chopped
    coriander roots and stems
1 tablespoon grated palm sugar
1/3 cup (80 ml/2¾ fl oz) lime juice
2 tablespoons fish sauce
2 small red chillies, seeded,
    finely sliced

2 red Asian shallots, finely sliced
2 telegraph cucumbers, sliced into
    thin ribbons
1 cup (30 g/1 oz) fresh mint leaves
1 cup (90 g/3 oz) bean sprouts
1/4 cup (30 g/1 oz) chopped roasted
    peanuts

1 Heat the wok until very hot, add
1 tablespoon of the oil and swirl it
around to coat the side. Add half the
beef and cook for 1–2 minutes, or until
medium rare. Remove from the wok
and set aside. Repeat with the rest of
the beef.
2 Place the crushed garlic, coriander,
palm sugar, lime juice, fish sauce,
1/4 teaspoon ground white pepper and

1/4 teaspoon salt in a bowl, and stir
until all the sugar has dissolved. Add
the chilli and shallots and mix well.
3 Pour the sauce over the beef while
still hot, mix well, then cool to room
temperature.
4 In a separate bowl, toss together
the cucumber and mint leaves, and
refrigerate until required.
5 Place the cucumber and mint on a
serving platter, and top with the beef,
bean sprouts and roasted peanuts.
Serve immediately.

NUTRITION PER SERVE
Protein 22 g; Fat 13 g; Carbohydrate 7.5 g;
Dietary Fibre 2 g; Cholesterol 50 mg;
1041 kJ (248 Cal)

Small red chillies are the hottest type. Remove
the seeds and white membrane, and finely slice.

Pour the sauce over the hot stir-fried beef and
leave to cool.

Toss together the cucumber and mint leaves and
leave in the fridge.

CHICKEN AND CASHEW NUTS

Preparation time: 30 minutes
Total cooking time: 20 minutes
Serves 4–6

oil, for cooking
750 g (1½ lb) chicken thigh fillets,
    cut into strips (see NOTE)
2 egg whites, lightly beaten
½ cup (60 g/2 oz) cornflour
2 onions, thinly sliced
1 red capsicum, thinly sliced
200 g (6½ oz) broccoli,
    cut into bite-sized pieces
2 tablespoons soy sauce
2 tablespoons sherry
1 tablespoon oyster sauce
⅓ cup (50 g/1¾ oz) roasted cashews
4 spring onions, diagonally sliced

1 Heat the wok until very hot, add 1 tablespoon of the oil and swirl it around to coat the side. Dip about a quarter of the chicken strips into the egg white and then into the cornflour. Add to the wok and stir-fry for 3–5 minutes, or until the chicken is golden brown and just cooked. Drain on paper towels and repeat with the remaining chicken, reheating the wok and adding a little more oil each time.
2 Reheat the wok, add 1 tablespoon of the oil and stir-fry the onion, capsicum and broccoli over medium heat for 4–5 minutes, or until the vegetables have softened slightly. Increase the heat to high and add the soy sauce, sherry and oyster sauce. Toss the vegetables well in the sauce and bring to the boil.
3 Return the chicken to the wok and toss over high heat for 1–2 minutes to heat the chicken and make sure it is entirely cooked through. Season well with salt and freshly cracked pepper. Toss the cashews and spring onion through the chicken mixture, and serve immediately.

NUTRITION PER SERVE (6)
Protein 35 g; Fat 15 g; Carbohydrate 15 g;
Dietary Fibre 3 g; Cholesterol 60 mg;
1375 kJ (330 cal)

NOTE: When choosing chicken, buy free range if you can, as it has a better flavour and texture. Yellowish flesh indicates the chicken has been grain fed but is not necessarily free range.

Dip the chicken strips into the egg white, then into the cornflour.

Stir-fry the chicken in small batches until it is golden brown.

SATAY LAMB

Preparation time: 20 minutes
Total cooking time: 15 minutes
Serves 4–6

oil, for cooking
500 g (1 lb) lamb fillet, thinly sliced
1 onion, chopped
2 cloves garlic, crushed
2 teaspoons grated fresh ginger
1–2 red chillies, seeded and finely
   chopped
1 teaspoon ground cumin
1 teaspoon ground coriander
1/2 cup (125 g/4 oz) crunchy peanut
   butter
1 tablespoon soy sauce
2 tablespoons lemon juice
1/2 cup (125 ml/4 fl oz) coconut cream

1 Heat the wok until very hot, add
1 tablespoon oil and swirl it around
to coat the side. Stir-fry the lamb in
batches over high heat until it is well
browned and cooked, adding more
oil when necessary. Remove the lamb
from the wok and set aside.
2 Reheat the wok, add 1 tablespoon
of the oil and stir-fry the onion over
medium heat for 2–3 minutes, or until
soft and transparent. Stir in the garlic,
ginger, chilli, cumin and coriander,
and cook for 1 minute.
3 Stir in the peanut butter, soy sauce,
lemon juice, coconut cream and
1/2 cup (125 ml/4 fl oz) water. Slowly
bring to the boil. Return the lamb to
the wok and stir until heated through.

NUTRITION PER SERVE (6)
Protein 25 g; Fat 25 g; Carbohydrate 5 g;
Dietary Fibre 3 g; Cholesterol 55 mg;
1390 kJ (330 Cal)

Stir-fry the onion over medium heat until it is soft
and transparent.

Add the garlic, ginger, chilli, cumin and coriander
to the onion.

Add the peanut butter, soy sauce, lemon juice,
coconut cream and water to the wok.

CHILLI TEMPEH

Preparation time: 15 minutes
Total cooking time: 10 minutes
Serves 4

250 g (8 oz) tempeh
oil, for cooking
1 onion, cut into thin slices
150 g (5 oz) asparagus,
　　cut into short lengths
1 large carrot, cut into thick
　　matchsticks
125 g (4 oz) snow peas, chopped

425 g (14 oz) can baby corn, drained
2 tablespoons sweet chilli sauce
2 tablespoons kecap manis
2 tablespoons dry sherry

1 Drain the tempeh, pat dry with paper towels and cut into bite-sized pieces for stir-frying.
2 Heat the wok until very hot, add 2 tablespoons of the oil and swirl it around to coat the side. Stir-fry the tempeh in batches until crisp. Remove from the wok and set aside.
3 Reheat the wok, add a little more oil if necessary and stir-fry the onion for

1 minute. Add the asparagus, carrot and snow peas, and stir-fry for 2–3 minutes, or until the vegetables are just tender.
4 Return the fried tempeh to the wok and add the baby corn, sweet chilli sauce, kecap manis and sherry. Bring to the boil, then reduce the heat and simmer for 2 minutes. Toss well until heated through and serve.

NUTRITION PER SERVE
Protein 5 g; Fat 15 g; Carbohydrate 10 g;
Dietary Fibre 8 g; Cholesterol 0 mg;
1270 kJ (300 cal)

Peel the carrot, cut it into short lengths and then into thick matchsticks.

Drain the tempeh, dry it on paper towels and cut it into bite-sized pieces.

Stir-fry the pieces of tempeh in the hot oil until they are crisp.

EGGPLANT WITH HOT BEAN SAUCE

Preparation time: 20 minutes
Total cooking time: 15 minutes
Serves 4–6

1/4 cup (60 ml/2 fl oz) peanut oil
800 g (1 lb 10 oz) eggplant, cut into
    small cubes
4 spring onions, chopped
3 cloves garlic, crushed
1 tablespoon finely chopped fresh
    ginger
1 tablespoon hot bean paste

1/2 cup (125 ml/4 fl oz) vegetable
    stock
1/4 cup (60 ml/2 fl oz) Chinese rice
    wine
2 tablespoons rice vinegar
1 tablespoon tomato paste
2 teaspoons soft brown sugar
2 tablespoons soy sauce
1 teaspoon cornflour
2 tablespoons shredded basil

1 Heat a wok until very hot, add
1 tablespoon oil and swirl to coat.
Stir-fry the eggplant in batches for
3–4 minutes, or until browned.
Remove from the wok.

2 Reheat the wok, add the remaining
oil and stir-fry the spring onion, garlic,
ginger and bean paste for 30 seconds.
Add the stock, rice wine, rice vinegar,
tomato paste, sugar and soy and stir-
fry for 1 minute.
3 Mix the cornflour with 1 tablespoon
water, add to the wok and bring to the
boil. Return the eggplant to the wok
and stir-fry for 2–3 minutes to cook
through. Sprinkle with basil to serve.

NUTRITION PER SERVE (6)
Protein 2 g; Fat 10 g; Carbohydrate 5.5 g;
Dietary Fibre 3.5 g; Cholesterol 0 mg;
550 kJ (130 cal)

You don't need to peel eggplant before cooking it. Simply cut it into cubes.

Stir-fry the spring onion, garlic, ginger and bean paste for 30 seconds.

Add the stock, rice wine, rice vinegar, tomato paste, sugar and soy and stir-fry for 1 minute.

CARAMEL CORIANDER CHICKEN

Preparation time: 20 minutes
  + overnight refrigeration
Total cooking time: 20 minutes
Serves 4–6

2 teaspoons ground turmeric
6 cloves garlic, crushed
2 tablespoons grated fresh ginger
2 tablespoons soy sauce
1/4 cup (60 ml/2 fl oz) Chinese rice
    wine or sherry
2 egg yolks, beaten
1 kg (2 lb) chicken thigh fillets,
    cut into cubes
1/2 cup (60 g/2 oz) plain flour
1/2 cup (125 ml/4 fl oz) oil

1/2 cup (90 g/3 oz) soft brown sugar
1/2 cup (30 g/1 oz) chopped coriander
1/4 cup (60 ml/2 fl oz) rice vinegar

1 Place the turmeric, 2 crushed garlic cloves, the ginger, soy, rice wine, egg yolks, 1 teaspoon salt and 1 teaspoon white pepper in a large bowl and mix together well. Add the chicken and toss to coat. Cover with plastic wrap and refrigerate overnight.
2 Pour away any excess liquid from the chicken, add the flour and toss to mix well.
3 Heat a wok until very hot, add 1 tablespoon oil and swirl to coat. Add a third of the chicken and stir-fry for 4 minutes, or until golden brown. Remove from the wok. Cook the other two batches of chicken, adding more

oil as necessary. Remove all the chicken from the wok and keep warm.
4 Reduce the heat to medium, add the remaining oil, brown sugar and remaining garlic. Mix together and then leave for 1–2 minutes, or until the sugar caramelizes and liquefies.
5 Return the chicken to the wok, and add the coriander and vinegar. Stir gently for 4 minutes, or until the chicken is cooked through and well coated with the sauce.

NUTRITION PER SERVE (6)
Protein 35 g; Fat 25 g; Carbohydrate 30 g;
Dietary Fibre 2 g; Cholesterol 130 mg;
2070 kJ (495 cal)

Cut the chicken thigh fillets into bite-sized cubes for even stir-frying.

Mix together the turmeric, garlic, ginger, soy, rice wine, egg yolks, salt and pepper.

Leave the sauce to cook until the sugar caramelizes and liquifies.

MA POR TOFU

Preparation time: 15 minutes
 + 10 minutes marinating
Total cooking time: 15 minutes
Serves 4

3 teaspoons cornflour
2 teaspoons soy sauce
1 teaspoon oyster sauce
1 clove garlic, finely chopped
250 g (8 oz) pork mince
1 tablespoon oil

3 teaspoons red bean chilli paste
3 teaspoons preserved bean curd
750 g (1¹/2 lb) firm tofu, drained,
   cubed
2 spring onions, sliced
3 teaspoons oyster sauce, extra
2 teaspoons soy sauce, extra
1¹/2 teaspoons sugar

1 Put the cornflour, soy and oyster sauces and the garlic in a bowl and mix well. Add the mince, toss to coat and leave for 10 minutes.
2 Heat a wok until very hot, add the oil and swirl to coat the base and side of the wok with oil. Add the mince and stir-fry for 5 minutes, or until browned. Add the chilli paste and bean curd, and cook for 2 minutes, or until fragrant.
3 Add the remaining ingredients and stir for 3–5 minutes, or until the tofu is heated through.

NUTRITION PER SERVE
Protein 26 g; Fat 12 g; Carbohydrate 5 g;
Dietary Fibre 0 g; Cholesterol 30 mg;
1092 kJ (260 Cal)

Drain the firm tofu from the liquid you buy it in, and cut it into cubes.

Add the minced pork to the cornflour, soy sauce, oyster sauce and garlic.

Stir-fry the pork mince until it is browned, then add the chilli paste and bean curd.

SESAME PORK

Preparation time: 10 minutes
Total cooking time: 20 minutes
Serves 4

2 tablespoons sesame seeds
3 tablespoons peanut oil
600 g (1¹/4 lb) pork fillets, thinly
   sliced
2 tablespoons hoisin sauce
2 tablespoons teriyaki sauce
2 teaspoons cornflour
2 teaspoons sesame oil
8 spring onions, sliced on the
   diagonal
2 cloves garlic, crushed

2 teaspoons finely grated fresh ginger
2 carrots, julienned
200 g (6¹/2 oz) snake beans, cut into
   short lengths

1 Preheat the oven to moderate 180°C (350°F/Gas 4). Place the sesame seeds on an oven tray and bake for 5 minutes, or until browned.
2 Heat a wok until very hot, add 1 tablespoon oil and swirl to coat. Add half the pork and stir-fry for 3 minutes, or until browned. Remove. Repeat with the remaining pork. Remove.
3 Combine the hoisin and teriyaki sauces, cornflour and 1 tablespoon water and mix until smooth.
4 Reheat the wok until very hot, add the remaining peanut oil and the sesame oil and swirl to coat. Add the spring onion, garlic and ginger, and stir-fry for 1 minute, or until fragrant.
5 Add the carrot and beans, and stir-fry for 3 minutes, or until almost cooked but still crunchy. Return the pork to the wok, add the cornflour mixture and stir until the sauce boils and thickens. Simmer until the meat is tender and the vegetables are just cooked. Toss through the sesame seeds and serve immediately.

NUTRITION PER SERVE
Protein 38 g; Fat 27 g; Carbohydrate 7.5 g;
Dietary Fibre 4.5 g; Cholesterol 75 mg;
1766 kJ (420 Cal)

Cut the snake beans into shorter lengths for easy stir-frying.

Cook the pork in two batches, so that it fries rather than stews.

Mix together the hoisin and teriyaki sauces, cornflour and 1 tablespoon of water.

VEGETABLES STIR-FRIED IN COCONUT MILK

Preparation time: 20 minutes
Total cooking time: 15 minutes
Serves 4

2 tablespoons oil
2 cloves garlic, chopped
5 cm (2 inch) piece fresh ginger, grated
2 teaspoons green peppercorns
1 eggplant, diced
1 small sweet potato, diced

100 g (3½ oz) green beans, cut into short lengths
200 g (6½ oz) asparagus, cut into short lengths
½ cup (125 ml/4 fl oz) coconut milk
2 teaspoons fish sauce
12 English spinach leaves, trimmed
½ cup (15 g/½ oz) Thai basil leaves

1 Heat the oil in a wok. Add the garlic, ginger and peppercorns and stir-fry for 30 seconds. Add the eggplant, sweet potato and 2 teaspoons water and stir-fry over medium heat for 5 minutes.

2 Add the beans to the wok, cover and steam for 4 minutes, shaking the wok occasionally to prevent the vegetables sticking.

3 Add the asparagus and coconut milk to the wok and stir-fry for 3 minutes or until the asparagus is just tender. Add the sauce, spinach and basil and toss until softened slightly. Serve immediately.

NUTRITION PER SERVE
Protein 3.5 g; Fat 16 g; Carbohydrate 10 g;
Dietary Fibre 4 g; Cholesterol 0 mg;
826 kJ (197 cal)

Add the diced eggplant, sweet potato and water to the wok. Cook for 5 minutes.

Cover the wok after adding the beans and steam the vegetables for 4 minutes.

Use two spoons to toss briefly until the spinach and basil have softened slightly.

BLACK BEAN AND CHILLI MUSSELS

Preparation time: 10 minutes
Total cooking time: 8 minutes
Serves 4

3 teaspoons salted black beans, rinsed
1 tablespoon shredded fresh ginger
2 cloves garlic, chopped
1 tablespoon sugar
2 tablespoons oyster sauce
1 teaspoon soy sauce
2 teaspoons oil
1 small red chilli, seeded and thinly sliced
1.2 kg (2 lb 6 oz) black mussels, scrubbed, debearded (see NOTE)
2 teaspoons cornflour
4 spring onions, sliced on the diagonal
coriander leaves, to serve

1 Place the black beans, ginger, garlic, sugar, oyster sauce and soy sauce in a small bowl and mash with a fork.
2 Heat a wok over high heat, add the oil and swirl to coat the side. Add the chilli and stir-fry for 30 seconds, then add the black bean mixture and stir-fry for 1 minute, or until fragrant. Add the mussels and stir-fry for 3–5 minutes, or until they open. Discard any that do not open. Reduce the heat to low.
3 Place the cornflour and $1/2$ cup (125 ml/4 fl oz) water in a bowl and stir until smooth. Add to the wok and bring to the boil, stirring until the sauce boils and thickens. Stir through the spring onion and coriander leaves.

NUTRITION PER SERVE
Protein 38 g; Fat 7.5 g; Carbohydrate 19 g; Dietary Fibre 1.5 g; Cholesterol 243 mg; 1240 kJ (295 Cal)

NOTE: When buying live mussels make sure they are fresh. Live mussels will have tightly closed shells—some may be slightly opened. Give the shells a tap and if they close this will indicate that they are still alive. Discard any with broken or cracked shells. Always buy extra to allow for the ones that are cracked or do not open during cooking.

Mash together the black beans, ginger, garlic, sugar, oyster and soy sauce.

Stir-fry the mussels for 3–5 minutes, or until they open. Discard any that don't open.

Add the cornflour mixture to the wok and bring to the boil until the sauce thickens.

THAI CHICKEN AND HOLY BASIL

Preparation time: 15 minutes
Total cooking time: 7 minutes
Serves 4

3 tablespoons fish sauce
3 tablespoons lime juice
1 tomato, diced
1 cup (30 g/1 oz) loosely packed Thai
    basil leaves
2 tablespoons peanut or vegetable oil
3 cloves garlic, thinly sliced
4 spring onions, finely sliced
2 small red chillies, seeded and thinly
    sliced
4 chicken breast fillets, thinly sliced
250 g (8 oz) snow peas, trimmed

1 Place the fish sauce, lime juice, tomato, basil and 1 tablespoon water in a small bowl and mix well.
2 Heat a wok over high heat, add the oil and swirl to coat the side. Add the garlic, spring onion and chilli and stir-fry for 1 minute, or until fragrant. Add the chicken and cook for 3 minutes, or until lightly browned.
3 Add the snow peas and the fish sauce mixture and scrape any bits from the bottom of the wok. Reduce the heat and simmer for 2 minutes, or until the tomato is soft and the chicken cooked through. Serve immediately.

NUTRITION PER SERVE
Protein 57 g; Fat 20 g; Carbohydrate 10 g;
Dietary Fibre 6.5 g; Cholesterol 110 mg;
1887 kJ (450 cal)

Mix together the fish sauce, lime juice, tomato, basil and water.

Add the chicken to the wok and stir-fry until it is lightly browned.

Simmer until the tomato is soft and the chicken is cooked through.

PORK WITH PUMPKIN AND CASHEW NUTS

Preparation time: 20 minutes
Total cooking time: 20 minutes
Serves 4

2–3 tablespoons oil
1/2 cup (90 g/3 oz) cashew nuts
750 g (1 1/2 lb) pork neck, cut into
    long, thin strips
500 g (1 lb) pumpkin, cubed
1 tablespoon grated fresh ginger
1/3 cup (80 ml/2 3/4 fl oz) chicken stock
1/4 cup (60 ml/2 fl oz) dry sherry

1 1/2 tablespoons soy sauce
1/2 teaspoon cornflour
500 g (1 lb) baby bok choy, chopped
1–2 tablespoons coriander leaves

1 Heat a wok until very hot, add 1 tablespoon oil and swirl to coat the side of the wok. Stir-fry the cashews for 1–2 minutes, or until browned. Drain on paper towels.

2 Reheat the wok, add a little extra oil and swirl to coat. Stir-fry the pork in batches for 5 minutes, or until lightly browned. Remove from the wok. Add 1 tablespoon oil to the wok and stir-fry the pumpkin and ginger for 3 minutes, or until lightly browned. Add the stock, sherry and soy sauce, and cook for 3 minutes, or until the pumpkin is tender.

3 Blend the cornflour with 1 teaspoon water until smooth, add to the wok and stir until the mixture boils and thickens. Return the pork and cashews to the wok and add the bok choy and coriander. Stir until the bok choy has just wilted. Serve immediately.

NUTRITION PER SERVE
Protein 46 g; Fat 28 g; Carbohydrate 15 g;
Dietary Fibre 8 g; Cholesterol 75 mg;
2112 kJ (505 cal)

Stir-fry the cashew nuts for 1–2 minutes, or until they are just browned.

Reheat the wok and brown the pork in batches so that it fries rather than stews.

Add the stock, sherry and soy sauce and cook until the pumpkin is tender.

LAMB WITH MIXED GREENS

Preparation time: 10 minutes
Total cooking time: 15 minutes
Serves 4

500 g (1 lb) lamb fillets, cut into strips about 2.5 cm (1 inch) wide
1 egg white, lightly beaten
1 tablespoon cornflour
2–3 tablespoons oil
2.5 cm (1 inch) piece fresh ginger, thinly sliced
2 cloves garlic, crushed
2 tablespoons soy sauce
2 leeks, finely sliced
250 g (8 oz) baby English spinach leaves, torn
1 small bunch bok choy, cut into short lengths
3/4 cup (115 g/4 oz) frozen peas
1 teaspoon sugar
3 tablespoons chicken stock
dash of chilli sauce

1 Season the strips of lamb with salt and pepper, dip in the egg white and dust with cornflour.
2 Heat half the oil in a wok and add the ginger, garlic and soy sauce. Stir-fry over high heat for 30 seconds. Add the lamb and stir-fry for 1 minute or until browned. Reduce the heat, cover and cook for 3 minutes. Remove the lamb from the wok.
3 Heat the remaining oil in the wok and add the leek. Stir-fry over high heat for 3 minutes, or until the leek has softened.
4 Add the spinach, bok choy and frozen peas to the wok and stir-fry for 1 minute. Reduce the heat and cover the wok to steam the vegetables for 2 minutes. Combine the sugar, stock and chilli sauce and add to the wok. Add the lamb and stir well. Stir-fry for 2 minutes or until the lamb and vegetables are just tender.

NUTRITION PER SERVE
Protein 35 g; Fat 30 g; Carbohydrate 7 g;
Dietary Fibre 5 g; Cholesterol 100 mg;
1775 kJ (425 cal)

Season the meat with salt and pepper, then dip in the egg white and cornflour.

Add the spinach, bok choy and frozen peas to the wok and stir-fry for 1 minute.

LEMON GRASS PRAWNS

Preparation time: 30 minutes
Total cooking time: 10 minutes
Serves 4

1 tablespoon peanut oil
2 cloves garlic, crushed
1 tablespoon finely grated fresh ginger
2 tablespoons finely chopped lemon
    grass, white part only
8 spring onions, cut into short lengths
1 kg (2 lb) raw prawns, peeled,
    deveined, tails intact

2 tablespoons lime juice
1 tablespoon soft brown sugar
2 teaspoons fish sauce
1/4 cup (60 ml/2 fl oz) chicken stock
1 teaspoon cornflour
500 g (1 lb) baby bok choy, cut in half
    lengthways
1/4 cup (15 g/1/2 oz) chopped mint

1 Heat a wok until very hot, add the oil and swirl to coat. Add the garlic, ginger, lemon grass and spring onion, and stir-fry for 1 minute, or until fragrant. Add the prawns and stir-fry for 2 minutes.

2 Place the lime juice, sugar, fish sauce, chicken stock and cornflour in a small bowl. Mix well, then add to the wok and stir until the sauce boils and thickens. Cook for a further 1–2 minutes, or until the prawns are pink and just tender.

3 Add the bok choy and stir-fry for 1 minute, or until wilted. Stir in the mint and serve.

NUTRITION PER SERVE
Protein 60 g; Fat 8.5 g; Carbohydrate 8 g;
Dietary Fibre 1.6 g; Cholesterol 373 mg;
1433 kJ (342 cal)

Peel the prawn bodies and heads, remove the dark veins, but leave the tail shells on.

Rinse the bok choy thoroughly and then slice in half down the middle.

Stir-fry the flavourings until they are fragrant, then add the prawns.

CHICKEN WITH BEANS AND ASPARAGUS

Preparation time: 25 minutes
+ 15 minutes marinating
Total cooking time: 15 minutes
Serves 4

1 stem lemon grass, white part only, chopped
5 cm (2 inch) piece ginger, peeled and chopped
2–3 small red chillies, seeded and chopped
1 teaspoon grated kaffir lime or lime rind
2–3 cloves garlic, chopped
1/2 teaspoon ground black pepper
2 tablespoons oil
375 g (12 oz) chicken breast fillets, cut into thin strips
250 g (8 oz) green beans, cut into short pieces
1 celery stick, cut into thick slices
185 g (6 oz) snow peas, halved
200 g (61/2 oz) asparagus, cut into short pieces
270 ml (9 fl oz) can coconut cream
2 tablespoons sweet chilli sauce
20 small fresh basil leaves

1 Place the lemon grass, ginger, chilli, lime rind, garlic, pepper and oil in a food processor or blender, and process until the mixture forms a rough paste. Combine the paste and chicken strips in a glass or ceramic bowl, cover and refrigerate for at least 15 minutes.
2 Briefly blanch the beans, celery, snow peas and asparagus in a pan of boiling water. Drain and plunge into iced water. Drain again.
3 Heat the wok until very hot and stir-fry the chicken mixture in batches over high heat for 3–4 minutes, or until the chicken is cooked through. Stir constantly so the paste doesn't burn. Return all of the chicken to the wok with the vegetables, coconut cream, sweet chilli sauce, to taste, and basil leaves. Stir-fry until heated through. Serve with rice or noodles.

NUTRITION PER SERVE
Protein 50 g; Fat 30 g; Carbohydrate 8 g;
Dietary Fibre 6 g; Cholesterol 95 mg;
1990 kJ (475 cal)

Grating rind is easier if you fit a piece of baking paper over the grater first.

Process the lemon grass, ginger, chilli, lime rind, garlic, pepper and oil to a paste.

grills & barbecues

BEEF TERIYAKI WITH CUCUMBER SALAD

Preparation time: 20 minutes +
    30 minutes refrigeration +
    10 minutes resting
Total cooking time: 20 minutes
Serves 4

4 scotch fillet steaks
1/3 cup (80 ml/2 3/4 fl oz) soy sauce
2 tablespoons mirin
1 tablespoon sake (optional)
1 clove garlic, crushed
1 teaspoon grated fresh ginger
1 teaspoon sugar
1 teaspoon toasted sesame seeds

CUCUMBER SALAD
1 large Lebanese cucumber, peeled,
    seeded and diced
1/2 red capsicum, diced
2 spring onions, sliced thinly on
    the diagonal
2 teaspoons sugar
1 tablespoon rice wine vinegar

1 Place the steaks in a non-metallic dish. Combine the soy, mirin, sake, garlic and ginger and pour over the steaks. Cover with plastic wrap and refrigerate for at least 30 minutes.
2 To make the cucumber salad, place the cucumber, capsicum and spring onion in a small bowl. Place the sugar, rice wine vinegar and 1/4 cup (60 ml/ 2 fl oz) water in a small saucepan and stir over medium heat until the sugar dissolves. Increase the heat and simmer rapidly for 3–4 minutes, or until slightly thickened. Pour over the cucumber salad, stir to combine and leave to cool completely.
3 Spray a chargrill or barbecue hot plate with oil spray and heat until very hot. Drain the steaks and reserve the marinade. Cook for 3–4 minutes on each side, or until cooked to your liking. Remove and rest the meat for 5–10 minutes before slicing.
4 Meanwhile, place the sugar and the reserved marinade in a small saucepan and heat, stirring, until the sugar has dissolved. Bring to the boil, then simmer for 2–3 minutes, remove from the heat and keep warm.
5 Slice each steak into 1 cm (1/2 inch) strips, being careful to keep the steak in its shape. Arrange the steak on each plate. Spoon on some of the marinade, a spoonful of cucumber salad and garnish with sesame seeds. Serve with steamed rice and the remaining cucumber salad.

NUTRITION PER SERVE
Protein 23 g; Fat 5 g; Carbohydrate 6 g; Dietary Fibre 1 g; Cholesterol 67 mg; 720 kJ (170 Cal)

Combine the cucumber, capsicum and spring onion with the dressing.

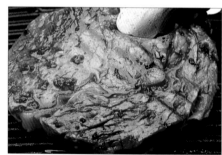

Cook the steaks for 3–4 minutes on each side, or until cooked to your liking.

SESAME CHICKEN KEBABS

Preparation time: 10 minutes +
   2 hours marinating
Total cooking time: 10 minutes
Serves 4

3 tablespoons oil
2 tablespoons soy sauce
2 tablespoons honey
1 tablespoon grated fresh ginger
1 tablespoon sesame oil
4 large chicken breast fillets, cubed
8 spring onions, cut into short lengths
1 tablespoon toasted sesame seeds
   (see HINT)

1 Soak 12 wooden skewers in water
to prevent scorching. To make the
marinade, whisk together the oil, soy
sauce, honey, ginger and sesame oil.

Thread the chicken and spring onion
onto the skewers and put in a non-
metallic dish. Add the marinade, cover
and refrigerate for at least 2 hours.
2 Place the skewers on a hot, lightly
oiled barbecue flatplate or grill and
baste with the remaining marinade.
Cook for 4 minutes on each side, or
until the chicken is cooked through.
Sprinkle with the sesame seeds.

Spread the pieces of chicken and spring onion
alternately onto the skewers.

NUTRITION PER SERVE
Protein 55 g; Fat 25 g; Carbohydrate 13 g;
Dietary Fibre 1 g; Cholesterol 120 mg;
2180 kJ (520 cal)

HINT: To toast sesame seeds, place in
a dry pan and shake over moderate
heat until golden.

Once the kebabs are cooked through, sprinkle
with the sesame seeds to serve.

FISH WRAPPED IN BANANA LEAVES

Preparation time: 20 minutes
Total cooking time: 35 minutes
Serves 4–6

SPICE PASTE
1 red onion, finely chopped
3 small red chillies, seeded and
    chopped
1 teaspoon dried shrimp paste
1 cm (1/2 inch) piece fresh galangal,
    finely chopped
1 stem lemon grass, white part only,
    finely sliced
5 blanched almonds, chopped
4 kaffir lime leaves, finely shredded

2 teaspoons sesame oil
1 tablespoon vegetable oil
1 teaspoon soy sauce
1 banana leaf (about 50 x 30 cm/
    20 x 12 inches)
1 whole trout or silver bream
    (about 750 g/1¹/2 lb),
    cleaned and scaled

1 To make the spice paste, grind all
the ingredients except the kaffir lime
leaves in a food processor with
2 tablespoons water until smooth.
Transfer to a bowl and mix in the kaffir
lime leaves. Set aside.
2 Heat the sesame oil and vegetable
oil in a small frying pan and gently fry
the paste for 5 minutes. Mix in the soy
sauce. Remove from the heat and cool.
3 Cut a large rectangle from the
banana leaf and brush with oil. Score
the fish several times on both sides
and rub in the paste, pushing it well
into the cuts.
4 Place the fish on the banana leaf
and fold over to make a parcel. Wrap
again in foil to secure and protect.
Cook over medium heat on a hot,
lightly oiled barbecue grill or flatplate
for 20–30 minutes, or until the flesh
flakes easily when tested with a fork.

NUTRITION PER SERVE (6)
Protein 30 g; Fat 15 g; Carbohydrate 3 g;
Dietary Fibre 1 g; Cholesterol 75 mg;
1050 kJ (250 cal)

Add the shredded kaffir lime leaves to the smooth
spice paste.

Stir the soy sauce into the fried spice paste and
mix well.

Score the fish several times on both sides with a
sharp knife.

Wrap the fish in the banana leaf, folding the ends
securely to make a parcel.

LAMB SATAYS WITH CHILLI PEANUT SAUCE

Preparation time: 25 minutes +
 1 hour marinating
Total cooking time: 15 minutes
Serves 4

600 g (1 1/4 lb) lamb fillet
2 cloves garlic, crushed
1/2 teaspoon ground black pepper
6 teaspoons finely chopped lemon
 grass
2 tablespoons soy sauce
2 teaspoons sugar
1/4 teaspoon ground turmeric

CHILLI PEANUT SAUCE
1 1/2 cups (250 g/8 oz) unsalted
 roasted peanuts
2 tablespoons vegetable oil
1 onion, roughly chopped
1 clove garlic, roughly chopped
1 tablespoon sambal oelek
1 tablespoon soft brown sugar
1 tablespoon kecap manis
 or soy sauce
1 teaspoon grated fresh ginger
1 1/2 teaspoons ground coriander
1 cup (250 ml/8 fl oz) coconut cream
1/4 teaspoon ground turmeric

1 Trim the lamb, cut into thin strips and thread onto skewers, bunching along three-quarters of the length. Place in a shallow non-metallic dish. Mix together the garlic, pepper, lemon grass, soy sauce, sugar and turmeric and brush over the meat. Leave to marinate for 1 hour.
2 To make the chilli peanut sauce, roughly grind the peanuts in a food processor for 10 seconds. Heat the oil in a small pan. Add the onion and garlic and cook over medium heat for

3–4 minutes or until translucent. Add the sambal oelek, sugar, kecap manis, ginger and coriander. Cook, stirring, for 2 minutes. Add the coconut cream, turmeric and ground peanuts. Reduce the heat and cook for 3 minutes, or until thickened. Season well and then process for 20 seconds, or until the sauce is almost smooth.
3 Cook the skewers on a hot, lightly oiled barbecue grill or flatplate for 2–3 minutes on each side.

NUTRITION PER SERVE
Protein 51 g; Fat 57 g; Carbohydrate 16 g;
Dietary Fibre 7 g; Cholesterol 99 mg;
3241 kJ (774 cal)

STORAGE: Satays can be marinated for up to 2 days, covered in the fridge. The sauce will keep for 3–4 days in a screw-top jar in the fridge.

Thread the strips of lamb onto the skewers and then marinate for 1 hour.

Coarsely grind the peanuts in a processor and then heat with the other sauce ingredients.

Process the sauce until it is almost smooth and then serve with the skewers.

MIRIN AND SAKE CHICKEN

Preparation time: 10 minutes +
  15 minutes marinating
Total cooking time: 10 minutes
Serves 4

4 large chicken breast fillets
2 tablespoons mirin
2 tablespoons sake

1 tablespoon oil
5 cm (2 inch) piece of fresh ginger,
  very finely sliced
3 teaspoons soy sauce

1 Put the chicken in a non-metallic dish. Combine the mirin, sake and oil and pour over the chicken. Marinate for 15 minutes, then drain the chicken, reserving the marinade.
2 Cook the chicken on a hot, lightly oiled barbecue grill or flatplate for

4 minutes on each side, or until tender.
3 Put the ginger in a pan and add the reserved marinade. Boil for about 7 minutes, or until thickened.
4 Drizzle the soy sauce over the chicken and top with the ginger. Serve immediately.

NUTRITION PER SERVE
Protein 35 g; Fat 10 g; Carbohydrate 1 g;
Dietary Fibre 0 g; Cholesterol 80 mg;
995 kJ (235 cal)

Put the chicken in a shallow, non-metallic dish and leave to marinate.

Cook the chicken for 4 minutes on each side, or until tender.

Put the ginger in a pan and add the reserved marinade. Boil until thickened.

SALMON AND PRAWN KEBABS WITH CHINESE SPICES

Preparation time: 15 minutes +
  2 hours marinating
Total cooking time: 20 minutes
Serves 6

4 x 200 g (6½ oz) salmon fillets
36 raw prawns, peeled, deveined, tails
  intact
5 cm (2 inch) piece fresh ginger, finely
  shredded
⅔ cup (170 ml/5½ fl oz) Chinese rice
  wine
¾ cup (185 ml/6 fl oz) kecap manis
½ teaspoon five-spice powder

200 g (6½ oz) fresh egg noodles
600 g (1¼ lb) baby bok choy, leaves
  separated

1 Remove the skin and bones from
the salmon and cut it into bite-sized
cubes (you should have about 36).
Thread three cubes of salmon
alternately with three prawns onto
each skewer. Lay the skewers in a
non-metallic dish.
2 Mix together the ginger, rice wine,
kecap manis and five-spice powder.
Pour over the skewers, then cover and
marinate for at least 2 hours. Turn over
a few times to ensure even coating.
3 Drain, reserving the marinade.
Cook the skewers in batches on a hot,
lightly oiled barbecue flatplate or grill

for 4–5 minutes each side, or until they
are cooked through.
4 Meanwhile, place the noodles in a
bowl and cover with boiling water.
Leave for 5 minutes, or until tender,
then drain and keep warm. Place the
reserved marinade in a saucepan and
bring to the boil. Reduce the heat,
simmer and stir in the bok choy
leaves. Cook, covered, for 2 minutes,
or until just wilted.
5 Top the noodles with the bok choy,
then the kebabs. Spoon on the heated
marinade, season and serve.

NUTRITION PER SERVE
Protein 50 g; Fat 15 g; Carbohydrate 24 g;
Dietary Fibre 5 g; Cholesterol 246 mg;
1856 kJ (440 cal)

Mix together the marinade ingredients and pour
over the skewers.

Cook the skewers in batches on a hot barbecue
flatplate or grill.

Add the bok choy to the reserved marinade in
the pan, cover and cook until wilted.

SWEET CHILLI CHICKEN

Preparation time: 15 minutes +
  2 hours marinating
Total cooking time: 15 minutes
Serves 6

1 kg (2 lb) chicken thigh fillets
2 tablespoons lime juice
1/2 cup (125 ml/4 fl oz) sweet chilli
  sauce
1/4 cup (60 ml/2 fl oz) kecap manis
  (see NOTE)

1 Trim any excess fat from the chicken thigh fillets and cut them in half. Transfer the pieces to a shallow, non-metallic dish.
2 Place the lime juice, sweet chilli sauce and kecap manis in a bowl and whisk to combine.
3 Pour the marinade over the chicken, cover and refrigerate for 2 hours.
4 Chargrill for 10–15 minutes, turning once, or until the chicken is tender and cooked through and the marinade has caramelised.

NUTRITION PER SERVE
Protein 35 g; Fat 4.5 g; Carbohydrate 4 g;
Dietary Fibre 1 g; Cholesterol 85 mg;
880 kJ (210 Cal)

NOTE: Kecap manis (ketjap manis) is a thick Indonesian sauce, similar to—but sweeter than—soy sauce, and is generally flavoured with garlic and star anise. Store in a cool, dry place and refrigerate after opening. If not available, use soy sauce sweetened with a little soft brown sugar.

Trim the excess fat from the thigh fillets, and cut them in half.

To make the marinade, whisk together the lime juice, sweet chilli sauce and kecap manis.

Pour the marinade over the chicken, then cover and refrigerate.

THAI-STYLE STUFFED CALAMARI TUBES

Preparation time: 30 minutes
Total cooking time: 10 minutes
Serves 4

8 very small calamari tubes (see NOTE)
2 tablespoons oil
4 cloves garlic, chopped
2 stems lemon grass, finely chopped
4 coriander roots, chopped
1–2 teaspoons Thai green curry paste
125 g (4 oz) pork mince
100 g (3½ oz) chicken mince
2 tablespoons fish sauce
2 tablespoons rice flour
1 tablespoon Golden Mountain sauce
2 teaspoons soft brown sugar
chilli sauce, to serve

1 Pull the tentacles from the body of the calamari. Pull the quill from the pouch of the calamari. Pull the skin away from the flesh and discard it. Wash the tubes thoroughly.
2 Heat half the oil in a frying pan over medium heat. Add the garlic, lemon grass, coriander root and curry paste and stir-fry for 2 minutes. Remove from the heat; add both the minces, the fish sauce and rice flour and mix well.
3 Fill each tube with the mixture and secure the end with a toothpick. Mix together the Golden Mountain sauce, sugar and 1 tablespoon water and brush over the tubes.
4 Brush a barbecue flatplate with the remaining oil and then heat to very hot. Add the tubes and cook, turning frequently, for 4–6 minutes or until just firm to the touch. Leave for 2 minutes before slicing, or serve whole. Serve with chilli sauce.

NUTRITION PER SERVE
Protein 74 g; Fat 15 g; Carbohydrate 9 g; Dietary Fibre 1 g; Cholesterol 744 mg; 1974 kJ (472 cal)

NOTE: Don't use pre-cleaned calamari as the tip will have been removed and the stuffing will come out. Baby calamari is very tender and only about 8 cm (3 inches) long.

Hold one end of the calamari, pull the skin away from the flesh and discard it.

Remove the frying pan from the heat and stir in the minces, fish sauce and rice flour.

Secure the ends of the filled calamari tubes with toothpicks so the filling won't come out.

Leave the cooked tubes for 2 minutes before slicing, or serve them whole.

CHICKEN TIKKA KEBABS

Preparation time: 10 minutes +
  2 hours marinating
Total cooking time: 10 minutes
Serves 4

10 chicken thigh fillets, cubed
1 red onion, cut into wedges
3 tablespoons tikka paste
1/2 cup (125 ml/4 fl oz) coconut milk
2 tablespoons lemon juice

1 Soak 8 skewers in water to prevent scorching. Thread 2 pieces of chicken and a wedge of onion alternately along each skewer. Place the skewers in a shallow, non-metallic dish.
2 Combine the tikka paste, coconut milk and lemon juice in a jar with a lid. Season and shake well to combine. Pour the mixture over the skewers and marinate for at least 2 hours, or overnight if time permits.
3 Cook the skewers on a hot, lightly oiled barbecue grill or flatplate for 4 minutes on each side, or until the chicken is cooked through. Put any leftover marinade in a small pan and bring to the boil. Serve as a sauce with the tikka kebabs.

NUTRITION PER SERVE
Protein 50 g; Fat 13 g; Carbohydrate 4 g;
Dietary Fibre 1.5 g; Cholesterol 114 mg;
1457 kJ (350 cal)

Thread a couple of pieces of chicken and then a wedge of onion and repeat until the skewer is full.

Mix the tikka marinade in a screw-top jar and then pour over the kebabs.

Cook the kebabs on a barbecue grill or flatplate until the chicken is cooked through.

TERIYAKI TUNA WITH WASABI MAYONNAISE AND PICKLED GINGER

Preparation time: 10 minutes +
   10 minutes marinating
Total cooking time: 10 minutes
Serves 4

1/2 cup (125 ml/4 fl oz) teriyaki
   marinade
1/2 teaspoon five-spice powder
1 tablespoon grated fresh ginger

3 tuna steaks, each cut into 4 strips
1/4 cup (60 g/2 oz) mayonnaise
1 teaspoon wasabi paste
2 tablespoons pickled ginger, to serve

1 Combine the teriyaki marinade, five-spice powder and ginger. Place the tuna in a non-metallic dish, pour over the marinade, cover and leave to marinate for 10 minutes. Drain and discard the marinade.

2 Cook the tuna, in batches if necessary, on a very hot, lightly oiled barbecue flatplate for 1–2 minutes

each side, or until cooked to your taste. Cooking time will vary depending on the thickness of the tuna steaks.

3 Mix together the mayonnaise and wasabi paste and serve with the tuna steaks, garnished with pickled ginger.

NUTRITION PER SERVE
Protein 27 g; Fat 17 g; Carbohydrate 4 g;
Dietary Fibre 0 g; Cholesterol 50 mg;
1196 kJ (284 cal)

Put the pieces of tuna in a shallow, non-metallic dish and add the marinade.

Cook the tuna on a very hot flatplate until it is cooked to your taste.

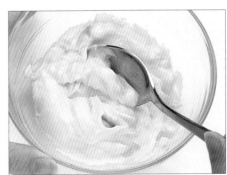

Mix together the mayonnaise and wasabi paste to serve with the tuna.

MALAYSIAN BARBECUED SEAFOOD

Preparation time: 30 minutes +
    15 minutes marinating
Total cooking time: 10 minutes
Serves 6

1 onion, grated
4 cloves garlic, chopped
5 cm (2 inch) piece of fresh ginger,
    grated
3 stems lemon grass (white
    part only), chopped
2 teaspoons ground or grated fresh
    turmeric
1 teaspoon shrimp paste
1/3 cup (80 ml/2³/4 fl oz) vegetable oil
1/4 teaspoon salt
4 medium calamari tubes
2 thick white boneless fish fillets
8 raw king prawns
banana leaves, for serving
2 limes, cut into wedges

1 Combine the onion, garlic, ginger, lemon grass, turmeric, shrimp paste, oil and salt in a small food processor. Process in short bursts until the mixture forms a paste.
2 Cut the calamari in half lengthways and lay it on the bench with the soft inside facing up. Score a very fine honeycomb pattern into the soft side,

taking care not to cut all the way through, and then cut into large pieces. Wash all the seafood under cold running water and pat dry with paper towels. Brush the seafood lightly with the spice paste. Place the seafood on a tray, cover and refrigerate for 15 minutes.
3 Lightly oil a barbecue hotplate and heat. When the plate is hot, arrange the fish fillets and prawns side by side on the plate. Cook for about 3 minutes on each side, turning them once only, or until the fish flesh is just firm and the prawns turn bright pink to orange. Add the calamari pieces and cook for about 2 minutes or until the flesh turns white and rolls up—take care not to overcook the seafood.
4 Arrange the seafood on a platter lined with the banana leaves, add the lime wedges and serve immediately, garnished with strips of lime rind and some fresh mint, if you like.

NUTRITION PER SERVE
Protein 33 g; Fat 3 g; Carbohydrate 1 g;
Dietary Fibre 1 g; Cholesterol 300 mg;
681 kJ (163 cal)

NOTE: Banana leaves are available from speciality fruit and vegetable shops. Alternatively, make friends with someone who has a banana tree.

Process in short bursts until the mixture forms a paste for coating the seafood.

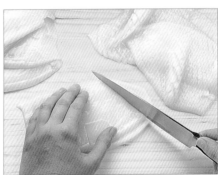

Score a fine honeycomb pattern into the soft side of the calamari.

SWEET-AND-SOUR PORK KEBABS

Preparation time: 30 minutes +
  3 hours marinating
Total cooking time: 20 minutes
Serves 6

1 kg (2 lb) pork fillets, cubed
1 large red capsicum, cubed
1 large green capsicum, cubed
425 g (14 oz) can pineapple pieces,
  drained, juice reserved
1 cup (250 ml/8 fl oz) orange juice
3 tablespoons white vinegar
2 tablespoons soft brown sugar
2 teaspoons chilli garlic sauce
2 teaspoons cornflour

1 Soak wooden skewers in water for 30 minutes to prevent scorching. Thread pieces of meat alternately with pieces of capsicum and pineapple onto the skewers. Mix the pineapple juice with the orange juice, vinegar, sugar and sauce. Place the kebabs in a shallow non-metallic dish and pour half the marinade over them. Cover and refrigerate for at least 3 hours, turning occasionally.
2 Put the remaining marinade in a small pan. Mix the cornflour with a tablespoon of the marinade until smooth, then add to the pan. Stir over medium heat until the mixture boils and thickens. Transfer to a bowl, cover the surface with plastic wrap and leave to cool.
3 Cook the kebabs on a hot, lightly oiled barbecue flatplate or grill for 15 minutes, turning occasionally, until tender. Serve with the sauce.

NUTRITION PER SERVE
Protein 40 g; Fat 3 g; Carbohydrate 18 g;
Dietary Fibre 2 g; Cholesterol 82 mg;
1073 kJ (256 cal)

Thread pieces of pork onto the skewers, alternating with capsicum and pineapple.

Mix the cornflour with a little of the marinade and then add to the sauce to thicken.

Cook the kebabs on a hot flatplate or grill until the pork is tender.

THAI BABY OCTOPUS

Preparation time: 1 hour
Total cooking time: 15–25 minutes
Serves 6

500 g (1 lb) baby octopus
2 tablespoons oil
3 cloves garlic, chopped
1 tablespoon green or pink
    peppercorns
2–4 small red chillies, finely chopped
1 tablespoon fish sauce

1 Cut off the octopus heads, below the eyes, with a sharp knife. Discard the heads and guts. Push the beaks out with your index finger, remove and discard. Wash the octopus thoroughly under running water and drain on crumpled paper towels. If the octopus tentacles are large, cut into quarters. Put in a shallow dish.

2 Mix together the oil, garlic, peppercorns and chilli, add to the octopus and marinate for 30 minutes. Cook 3 octopus at a time, turning frequently, on a very hot, lightly oiled barbecue grill or flatplate for 3 minutes or until they turn white. Do not overcook. Sprinkle the fish sauce over the top and serve immediately.

NUTRITION PER SERVE
Protein 14 g; Fat 7 g; Carbohydrate 0 g;
Dietary Fibre 0 g; Cholesterol 166 mg;
522 kJ (125 cal)

HINT: This recipe is also suitable for calamari. Wash the tubes, pat dry and cut into strips before marinating and cooking in the same way.

Use a sharp knife to slice off the head of the octopus so you can remove the gut.

Use your index finger to push the beak up so you can remove and discard it.

Cook the octopus, turning frequently, until they turn white.

THAI MEATBALL SKEWERS

Preparation time: 25 minutes
Total cooking time: 10 minutes
Serves 4

350 g (11 oz) beef mince
3 French shallots, finely chopped
3 cloves garlic, chopped
2.5 cm (1 inch) piece fresh ginger, grated
1 tablespoon green or pink peppercorns, crushed

2 teaspoons Golden Mountain sauce
2 teaspoons fish sauce
2 teaspoons soft brown sugar
lime wedges, to serve

1 Soak wooden skewers in water to prevent scorching. Chop the mince with a cleaver or large knife until the mince is very fine. Mix together the mince, French shallots, garlic, ginger, peppercorns, Golden Mountain sauce, fish sauce and brown sugar with your hands until well combined.

2 Using 2 teaspoons of mixture at a time, form into balls. Thread three of the balls onto each of the skewers.

3 Cook the skewers on a hot, lightly oiled barbecue grill or flatplate, turning frequently, for 7–8 minutes or until the meat is cooked. Serve with the lime wedges.

NUTRITION PER SERVE
Protein 78 g; Fat 10 g; Carbohydrate 4 g;
Dietary Fibre 1 g; Cholesterol 55 mg;
728 kJ (174 cal)

Use a large, sharp knife or a cleaver to chop the mince until very fine.

Form 2 teaspoonsful of mixture at a time into small, compact balls.

Cook the skewered meatballs, turning frequently, for 7–8 minutes.

CORIANDER PRAWNS

Preparation time: 15 minutes +
  30 minutes marinating
Total cooking time: 5 minutes
Serves 4

8 very large raw prawns
1 tablespoon sweet chilli sauce
1 teaspoon ground coriander
1/2 cup (125 ml/4 fl oz) olive oil
1/3 cup (80 ml/2³/₄ fl oz) lime juice
3 cloves garlic, crushed
1 tomato, peeled, seeded and
  chopped
2 tablespoons roughly chopped
  fresh coriander

1 Remove the heads from the prawns and, with a sharp knife, cut the prawns in half lengthways, leaving the tails attached. Pull out each dark vein.
2 Mix together the sweet chilli sauce and ground coriander with half the olive oil, half the lime juice and half the garlic. Add the prawns, toss to coat, then cover and marinate in the fridge for 30 minutes.
3 Meanwhile, to make the dressing, mix the remaining olive oil, lime juice and garlic in a bowl with the chopped tomato and fresh coriander.
4 Drain the prawns, reserving the marinade and cook, cut-side-down, on a hot, lightly oiled barbecue grill or flatplate for 1–2 minutes each side, or

until cooked through, brushing occasionally with the marinade.
5 Spoon a little of the dressing over the prawns and season well before serving.

NUTRITION PER SERVE
Protein 42 g; Fat 31 g; Carbohydrate 2.5 g;
Dietary Fibre 2 g; Cholesterol 298 mg;
1930 kJ (460 cal)

Cut each prawn through the centre lengthways, leaving the tail attached.

Stir the dressing ingredients together in a bowl until well combined.

Cook both sides of the drained prawns on a hot barbecue grill.

THAI CHICKEN CUTLETS

Preparation time: 20 minutes
  + 1 hour marinating
Total cooking time: 20 minutes
Serves 4–6

12 chicken thigh fillets (1.25 kg/2½ lb)
6 cloves garlic
1 teaspoon black peppercorns
3 fresh coriander roots and stems,
    roughly chopped
¼ teaspoon salt

CHILLI GARLIC DIP
4–5 dried red chillies
2 large cloves garlic, chopped
¼ cup (60 g/2 oz) sugar
⅓ cup (80 ml/2¾ fl oz) cider or rice
    vinegar
pinch salt
¼ cup (60 ml/2 fl oz) boiling water

1 Trim the chicken thigh fillets of any excess fat and sinew.
2 Place the garlic, peppercorns, coriander and salt in a food processor bowl. Process for 20–30 seconds, or until the mixture forms a smooth paste. (This can also be done using a mortar and pestle.) Place the chicken in a shallow non-metal dish. Spread the garlic mixture over the chicken. Refrigerate the chicken, covered, for 1 hour.
3 To make the chilli garlic dip, soak the chillies in hot water for 20 minutes. Drain the chillies and chop finely. Place in a mortar with the garlic and sugar, and grind to a smooth paste. Place the mixture in a small pan and add the vinegar, salt and boiling water. Bring to the boil, then reduce the heat and simmer for 2–3 minutes. Set aside to cool.
4 Preheat a barbecue grill or flatplate to high. Grease the barbecue and cook the chicken for 5–10 minutes on each side, turning once. Serve with the chilli garlic dip.

NUTRITION PER SERVE (6)
Protein 47 g; Fat 5 g; Carbohydrate 0.5 g;
Dietary Fibre 1 g; Cholesterol 105 mg;
1005 kJ (240 cal)

Using a sharp knife, trim any excess fat and sinew from the chicken.

Place the garlic, peppercorns, coriander and salt in a food processor bowl.

Grind the chilli, garlic and sugar to a smooth paste using a mortar and pestle.

Cook the chicken on a greased barbecue grill or flat plate.

INDIAN SEEKH KEBABS

Preparation time: 40 minutes
Total cooking time: 12 minutes
Serves 4

pinch of ground cloves
pinch of ground nutmeg
1/2 teaspoon chilli powder
1 teaspoon ground cumin
2 teaspoons ground coriander
3 cloves garlic, finely chopped
5 cm (2 inch) piece fresh ginger,
    grated
500 g (1 lb) lean beef mince
1 tablespoon oil
2 tablespoons lemon juice

ONION AND MINT RELISH
1 red onion, finely chopped
1 tablespoon white vinegar
1 tablespoon lemon juice
1 tablespoon chopped fresh mint

1 Soak 12 thick wooden skewers in cold water to prevent scorching. Dry-fry the cloves, nutmeg, chilli, cumin and coriander in a heavy-based frying pan, over low heat, for 2 minutes, shaking the pan constantly. Transfer to a bowl with the garlic and ginger and set aside.
2 Knead the mince firmly with your fingertips and the base of your hand for 3 minutes, or until very soft and a little sticky (this gives the kebabs the correct soft texture when cooked). Add the mince to the spice and garlic mixture and mix well, seasoning with plenty of salt and pepper.
3 Form tablespoons of the meat into small, round patties. Wet your hands and press two portions of the meat around a skewer, leaving a small gap at the top. Smooth the outside gently,

place on baking paper and refrigerate while making the remaining kebabs.
4 To make the relish, mix the onion, vinegar and lemon juice and refrigerate for 10 minutes. Stir in the mint and season with pepper.
5 Cook the skewers on a hot, lightly oiled barbecue grill or flatplate for about 8 minutes, turning regularly and sprinkling with a little lemon juice. Serve with the relish.

NUTRITION PER SERVE
Protein 16 g; Fat 13 g; Carbohydrate 2 g;
Dietary Fibre 1 g; Cholesterol 47 mg;
798 kJ (190 cal)

NOTE: These kebabs freeze very well —simply defrost before barbecuing.

Peel and chop the garlic and peel and grate the piece of fresh ginger.

Dry-fry the cloves, nutmeg, chilli, cumin and coriander in a heavy-based pan.

Form the meat mixture into small patties and then press two around each skewer.

curries & hotpots

Curry Pastes

Thai red and green curry pastes are those most commonly used for spicing up stir-fries, but the Panang curry paste is great for cooking chicken, and the musaman curry paste is traditionally used with beef.

RED CURRY PASTE

1 tablespoon coriander seeds
2 teaspoons cumin seeds
1 teaspoon black peppercorns
2 teaspoons dried shrimp paste
1 teaspoon ground nutmeg
12 dried or fresh red chillies, roughly chopped
4 French shallots, chopped
2 tablespoons oil
4 stems lemon grass (white part only), finely chopped
12 small cloves garlic, chopped
2 tablespoons coriander roots, chopped
2 tablespoons coriander stems, chopped
6 kaffir lime leaves, chopped
2 teaspoons grated lime rind
2 teaspoons salt
2 teaspoons turmeric
1 teaspoon paprika

Dry-fry the coriander and cumin seeds in a wok for 2–3 minutes, then finely grind in a mortar and pestle or spice grinder with the peppercorns. Wrap the shrimp paste in foil and cook under a hot grill (broiler) for 3 minutes, turning twice. Process the ground spices, roasted shrimp paste, nutmeg and chillies for 5 seconds. Add the remaining ingredients and process for 20 seconds at a time until you have a smooth paste. Makes 1 cup

GREEN CURRY PASTE

1 tablespoon coriander seeds
2 teaspoons cumin seeds
1 teaspoon black peppercorns
2 teaspoons dried shrimp paste
8 large fresh green chillies, roughly chopped
4 French shallots, chopped
5 cm (2 inch) piece fresh galangal, pounded or chopped
12 small cloves garlic, chopped
60 g (2 oz) chopped coriander leaves, stems and roots
6 kaffir lime leaves, chopped
3 stems lemon grass (white part only), finely chopped
2 teaspoons grated lime rind
2 teaspoons salt
2 tablespoons oil

Dry-fry the coriander and cumin seeds in a wok for 2–3 minutes, then finely grind in a mortar and pestle with the peppercorns. Wrap the shrimp paste in foil and cook under a hot grill (broiler) for 3 minutes, turning twice. Process the ground spices and shrimp paste for 5 seconds. Add the remaining ingredients and process for 20 seconds at a time until you have a smooth paste.
Makes 1 cup

PANANG CURRY PASTE

8 large dried red chillies
2 teaspoons shrimp paste
3 French shallots, chopped
5 cm (2 inch) piece fresh galangal, pounded or chopped
12 small cloves garlic, chopped
4 coriander roots, chopped
3 stems lemon grass (white part only), finely chopped
1 tablespoon grated lime rind
1 teaspoon black peppercorns
2 tablespoons oil
1 tablespoon fish sauce
1 teaspoon salt
1/2 cup (125 g/4 oz) crunchy peanut butter

Trim the stems from the chillies and soak them in 125 ml (4 fl oz) hot water for 30 minutes. Wrap the shrimp paste in foil and cook under a hot grill (broiler) for 2–3 minutes, turning the package twice. Place the softened chillies and soaking water, shrimp paste, shallots, galangal, garlic, coriander root, lemon grass, lime rind, peppercorns and oil in a food processor. Process for 20 seconds at a time, scraping down the side of the bowl with a spatula each time, until the mixture forms a smooth paste. Add the fish sauce, salt and peanut butter; process for 10 seconds or until combined. Makes approximately 1 cup

MUSAMAN CURRY PASTE

1 tablespoon coriander seeds
1 tablespoon cumin seeds
seeds from 4 cardamom pods
2 teaspoons black peppercorns
1 tablespoon shrimp paste
1 teaspoon grated nutmeg
1/2 teaspoon ground cloves
15 dried red chillies
3 French shallots, chopped
2 stems lemon grass (white part only), finely chopped
6 small cloves garlic, chopped
1 tablespoon oil

Dry-fry the coriander, cumin and cardamom seeds in a wok for 2–3 minutes. Place the spices and peppercorns in a mortar and pestle or spice grinder and finely grind. Place the ground spices and remaining ingredients in a food processor. Process for 20 seconds and scrape down the side of the bowl with a spatula. Process for 5 seconds at a time until the mixture forms a smooth paste.
Makes approximately 1 cup

GREEN CHICKEN CURRY

Preparation time: 20 minutes
Total cooking time: 25 minutes
Serves 4

1 tablespoon oil
1 onion, chopped
1–2 tablespoons green curry paste
1½ cups (375 ml/12 fl oz) coconut milk
500 g (1 lb) chicken thigh fillets, cut into bite-sized pieces
100 g (3½ oz) green beans, cut into short pieces
6 kaffir lime leaves
1 tablespoon fish sauce
1 tablespoon lime juice
1 teaspoon finely grated lime rind
2 teaspoons soft brown sugar
¼ cup (7 g/¼ oz) fresh coriander leaves

1 Heat the oil in a wok or a heavy-based pan. Add the onion and curry paste to the wok and cook for about 1 minute, stirring constantly. Add the coconut milk and ½ cup (125 ml/4 fl oz) water and bring to the boil.
2 Add the chicken pieces, beans and kaffir lime leaves to the wok, and stir to combine. Simmer, uncovered, for 15–20 minutes, or until the chicken is tender. Add the fish sauce, lime juice, lime rind and brown sugar to the wok, and stir to combine. Sprinkle with fresh coriander leaves just before serving. Serve with steamed rice.

NUTRITION PER SERVE
Protein 32 g; Fat 28 g; Carbohydrate 8 g;
Dietary Fibre 3 g; Cholesterol 63 mg;
1702 kJ (407 cal)

NOTE: Chicken thigh fillets are sweet in flavour and a very good texture for curries. You can use breast fillets instead, if you prefer. Do not overcook fillets or they will be tough.

Add the coconut milk and water to the wok and stir with a wooden spoon.

After simmering, stir in the fish sauce, lime juice, lime rind and brown sugar.

CHINESE BEEF IN SOY

Preparation time: 20 minutes +
  overnight marinating
Total cooking time:
  1 hour 45 minutes
Serves 4

700 g (1 lb 7 oz) chuck steak, trimmed
  and cut into 2 cm cubes
1/3 cup (80 ml/2³/4 fl oz) dark soy
  sauce
2 tablespoons honey
1 tablespoon wine vinegar
3 tablespoons soy bean oil
4 cloves garlic, chopped
8 spring onions, finely sliced

1 tablespoon finely grated fresh ginger
2 star anise
1/2 teaspoon ground cloves
1½ cups (375 ml/12 fl oz) beef stock
1/2 cup (125 ml/4 fl oz) red wine
spring onions, extra, sliced, to garnish

1 Place the meat in a non-metallic
dish. Combine the soy sauce, honey
and vinegar in a small bowl, then pour
over the meat. Cover with plastic wrap
and marinate for at least 2 hours, or
preferably overnight. Drain, reserving
the marinade, and pat the cubes dry.
2 Place 1 tablespoon of the oil in
a saucepan and brown the meat in
3 batches, for 3–4 minutes per batch—
add another tablespoon of oil, if

necessary. Remove the meat. Add the
remaining oil and fry the garlic, spring
onion, ginger, star anise and cloves for
1–2 minutes, or until fragrant.
3 Return all the meat to the pan,
add the reserved marinade, stock and
wine. Bring to the boil and simmer,
covered, for 1 hour 15 minutes. Cook,
uncovered, for a further 15 minutes,
or until the sauce is syrupy and the
meat is tender.
4 Garnish with the extra sliced spring
onion and serve immediately with rice.

NUTRITION PER SERVE
Protein 37 g; Fat 20 g; Carbohydrate 12 g;
Dietary Fibre 0.5 g; Cholesterol 117 mg;
1657 kJ (395 Cal)

Cook the cubes of beef, in batches, until brown all over.

Simmer the beef, marinade, stock and wine until the sauce is thick and syrupy.

Finely grate a piece of fresh ginger on a wooden ginger grater.

THAI PRAWN CURRY

Preparation time: 30 minutes
Total cooking time: 10 minutes
Serves 4

2 cm x 2 cm (3/4 inch x 3/4 inch) piece
   fresh galangal
1 small onion, roughly chopped
3 cloves garlic
4 dried long red chillies
4 whole black peppercorns
2 tablespoons chopped lemon
   grass, white part only
1 tablespoon chopped fresh coriander
   root
2 teaspoons grated lime rind

2 teaspoons cumin seeds
1 teaspoon sweet paprika
1 teaspoon ground coriander
3 tablespoons oil
1–2 tablespoons fish sauce
2 kaffir lime leaves
2 cups (500 ml/16 fl oz) coconut
   cream
1 kg (2 lb) raw medium prawns,
   peeled and deveined

1 Peel the galangal and thinly slice.
Process the onion, garlic, chillies,
peppercorns, lemon grass, coriander
root, lime rind, cumin seeds, paprika,
coriander, 2 tablespoons oil and
1/2 teaspoon salt in a small food
processor until a smooth paste forms.

2 Heat the remaining oil in a frying
pan. Add half the curry paste and
stir over medium heat for 2 minutes.
(Leftover curry paste can be kept in
the refrigerator for up to 2 weeks.)
Stir in the fish sauce, galangal, kaffir
lime leaves and coconut cream.
3 Add the prawns to the pan and
simmer for 5 minutes, or until the
prawns are cooked and the sauce has
thickened slightly. Serve with steamed
rice. Can be garnished with shredded
kaffir lime leaves and strips of chilli.

NUTRITION PER SERVE
Protein 42 g; Fat 39.5 g; Carbohydrate 9 g;
Dietary Fibre 4 g; Cholesterol 279.5 mg;
2310 kJ (550 Cal)

Peel the galangal and use a sharp knife to cut
into very thin slices.

Add half the curry paste to the pan and stir over
medium heat for 2 minutes.

Add the prawns to the pan and simmer until
cooked.

SRI LANKAN FRIED PORK CURRY

Preparation time: 45 minutes
Total cooking time: 1 hour 40 minutes
Serves 6

1/3 cup (80 ml/2 3/4 fl oz) oil
1.25 kg (2 1/2 lb) boned pork shoulder, cut into 3 cm (1 1/4 inch) cubes
1 large red onion, finely chopped
3–4 cloves garlic, crushed
1 tablespoon grated fresh ginger
10 curry leaves
1/2 teaspoon fenugreek seeds
1/2 teaspoon chilli powder
6 cardamom pods, bruised
2 tablespoons Sri Lankan curry powder
1 tablespoon white vinegar
1/3 cup (105 g/3 1/2 oz) tamarind concentrate
270 ml (9 fl oz) coconut cream

1 Heat half the oil in a large saucepan over high heat, add the meat and cook in batches for 6 minutes, or until well browned. Remove from the saucepan.
2 Heat the remaining oil in the saucepan, add the onion and cook over medium heat for 5 minutes, or until lightly browned. Add the garlic and ginger, and cook for 2 minutes.

Stir in the curry leaves, spices and curry powder, and cook for 2 minutes, or until fragrant. Stir in the vinegar and 1 teaspoon salt.
3 Return the meat to the pan, add the tamarind and 1 1/4 cups (315 ml/ 10 fl oz) water and simmer, covered, for 50 minutes, or until the meat is tender. Stir occasionally. Stir in the coconut cream and simmer, uncovered, for 15 minutes, or until the sauce reduces and thickens. Serve with rice.

NUTRITION PER SERVE
Protein 48 g; Fat 25 g; Carbohydrate 3 g; Dietary Fibre 1 g; Cholesterol 100 mg; 1800 kJ (430 Cal)

Cook the meat in batches for 6 minutes, or until well browned.

Cook the onion over medium heat until lightly browned.

Simmer, uncovered, until the sauce has reduced and thickened.

DUCK AND PINEAPPLE CURRY

Preparation time: 10 minutes
Total cooking time: 15 minutes
Serves 4–6

1 tablespoon peanut oil
8 spring onions, cut into short lengths
2 cloves garlic, crushed
1 tablespoon red curry paste
750 g (1¹/₂ lb) Chinese barbecued duck, chopped (see NOTE)

400 ml (13 fl oz) coconut milk
450 g (14 oz) can pineapple pieces in syrup, drained
3 kaffir lime leaves
¹/₄ cup (15 g/¹/₂ oz) chopped coriander
2 tablespoons chopped mint

1 Heat a wok until very hot, add the oil and swirl to coat. Add the spring onion, garlic and curry paste to the wok, and stir-fry for 1 minute, or until the paste is fragrant.
2 Add the remaining ingredients.

Bring to the boil, then reduce the heat and simmer for 10 minutes, or until the duck is heated through.

NUTRITION PER SERVE (6)
Protein 4 g; Fat 32 g; Carbohydrate 25 g;
Dietary Fibre 4.5 g; Cholesterol 10 mg;
1705 kJ (405 cal)

NOTE: You can chop the duck yourself if you have a cleaver, or ask for it to be done when you buy it.

Chop the barbecued duck into smaller pieces, or ask for this to be done when you buy it.

Cook the spring onion, garlic and curry paste for 1 minute, or until the paste is fragrant.

Add the remaining ingredients to the wok and simmer for 10 minutes.

LAMB KORMA

Preparation time: 30 minutes +
   1 hour marinating
Total cooking time: 1 hour 10 minutes
Serves 4–6

2 kg (4 lb) leg of lamb, boned
1 onion, chopped
2 teaspoons grated fresh ginger
3 cloves garlic
2 teaspoons ground coriander
2 teaspoons ground cumin
1 teaspoon cardamom seeds
large pinch cayenne pepper
2 tablespoons ghee or oil
1 onion, extra, sliced
2 1/2 tablespoons tomato paste
1/2 cup (125 g/4 oz) plain yoghurt
1/2 cup (125 ml/4 fl oz) coconut cream
1/2 cup (95 g/3 oz) ground almonds
toasted slivered almonds, to serve

1 Trim any excess fat or sinew from
the leg of lamb, then cut the meat into
3 cm (1 1/4 inch) cubes and place in a
large bowl.
2 Place the onion, ginger, garlic,
coriander, cumin, cardamom seeds,
cayenne pepper and 1/2 teaspoon salt

in a food processor, and process to a
smooth paste. Add the spice mixture
to the lamb and mix well to coat.
Leave to marinate for 1 hour.
3 Heat the ghee in a large saucepan,
add the extra sliced onion and cook,
stirring, over low heat for 7 minutes,
or until the onion is soft. Add the lamb
mixture and cook, stirring constantly,
for 8–10 minutes, or until the lamb
changes colour. Stir in the tomato
paste, yoghurt, coconut cream and
ground almonds.
4 Reduce the heat and simmer,
covered, stirring occasionally, for
50 minutes, or until the meat is
tender. Add a little water if the mixture
becomes too dry. Season with salt and
pepper, and garnish with the slivered
almonds. Serve with rice.

NUTRITION PER SERVE (6)
Protein 80 g; Fat 23 g; Carbohydrate 5 g;
Dietary Fibre 2 g; Cholesterol 240 mg;
2280 kJ (545 Cal)

NOTE: Korma curries can also be
made using beef or chicken. Korma
refers to the style of curry—rich and
smooth, and including almonds.

Trim any excess fat or sinew from the lamb and
cut into cubes.

Process the spice mixture until it forms a
smooth paste.

THAI RED PORK AND PUMPKIN CURRY

Preparation time: 20 minutes
Total cooking time: 25 minutes
Serves 4

1 tablespoon oil
1–2 tablespoons red curry paste
500 g (1 lb) lean pork, cubed
350 g (11 oz) butternut or Japanese
   pumpkin, peeled and cubed
6 kaffir lime leaves

1 cup (250 ml/8 fl oz) coconut milk
1/4 cup (60 ml/2 fl oz) coconut cream
1 tablespoon fish sauce
1 teaspoon soft brown sugar
2 red chillies, thinly sliced

1 Heat the oil in a wok, add the curry paste and stir for 1 minute.
2 Add the pork to the wok and stir-fry over medium–high heat until golden brown. Add the pumpkin, lime leaves, coconut milk and 1/2 cup (125 ml/ 4 fl oz) water, reduce the heat and simmer for 15 minutes, or until the pork is tender.
3 Add the coconut cream, fish sauce and brown sugar and stir to combine. Scatter chilli over the top to serve.

NUTRITION PER SERVE
Protein 30 g; Fat 11 g; Carbohydrate 9 g;
Dietary Fibre 1.5 g; Cholesterol 62 mg;
1085 kJ (260 Cal)

NOTE: Butternut and Japanese pumpkins are tender, sweet varieties.

Add the curry paste to the hot oil and stir with a wooden spoon for 1 minute.

Add the pork pieces to the wok and stir-fry over medium–high heat until golden brown.

Add the coconut cream, fish sauce and brown sugar to the wok and stir well.

CLAY-POT CHICKEN AND VEGETABLES

Preparation time: 20 minutes
  + 30 minutes marinating
Total cooking time: 25 minutes
Serves 4

500 g (1 lb) chicken thigh fillets
1 tablespoon soy sauce
1 tablespoon dry sherry
6 dried Chinese mushrooms
2 small leeks
250 g (8 oz) orange sweet potato
2 tablespoons peanut oil
5 cm (2 inch) piece ginger, shredded
1/2 cup (125 ml/4 fl oz) chicken stock
1 teaspoon sesame oil
3 teaspoons cornflour

1 Pat the chicken dry with paper towels. Cut into small pieces. Place in a dish with the soy sauce and sherry, cover and marinate for 30 minutes in the refrigerator.
2 Soak the mushrooms in hot water to cover for 30 minutes. Drain and squeeze to remove the excess liquid. Remove the stems and shred the caps.
3 Wash the leeks thoroughly to remove all the grit, then cut into thin slices. Cut the sweet potato into thin slices.
4 Drain the chicken, reserving the marinade. Heat half the peanut oil in a wok or heavy-based frying pan, swirling it gently to coat the base and side. Carefully add half the chicken pieces and stir-fry briefly until seared on all sides. Transfer to a flameproof clay pot or casserole. Stir-fry the remaining chicken and add to the clay pot.
5 Heat the remaining oil in a wok, add the leek and ginger and stir-fry for

1 minute. Add the mushrooms, the remaining marinade, the stock and sesame oil. Transfer to the clay pot, add the sweet potato and cook, covered, on the stove top over very low heat for about 20 minutes. Dissolve the cornflour with a little water and add to the pot. Cook, stirring, until the mixture boils and thickens. Serve the chicken and vegetables at once with steamed brown or white rice or with noodles.

NUTRITION PER SERVE
Protein 30 g; Fat 15 g; Carbohydrate 13 g;
Dietary Fibre 2.5 g; Cholesterol 60 mg;
1277 kJ (305 cal)

Wash the leeks to remove all the grit, then cut into thin slices.

Stir-fry the marinated chicken pieces until seared on all sides.

Add the mushrooms, marinade, stock and sesame oil to the leek mixture.

MALAY FISH CURRY

Preparation time: 25 minutes
Total cooking time: 25 minutes
Serves 4

3–6 red chillies, to taste
1 onion, chopped
4 cloves garlic
3 stems lemon grass, white part only,
    sliced
5 cm (2 inch) piece fresh ginger, sliced
2 teaspoons shrimp paste
1/4 cup (60 ml/2 fl oz) oil
1 tablespoon fish curry powder
    (see NOTE)
1 cup (250 ml/8 fl oz) coconut milk

1 tablespoon tamarind concentrate
1 tablespoon kecap manis
350 g (11 oz) firm white fish fillets,
    cut into bite-sized pieces
2 ripe tomatoes, chopped
1 tablespoon lemon juice

1 Combine the chillies, onion, garlic, lemon grass, ginger and shrimp paste in a small food processor and process until roughly chopped. Add 2 tablespoons of oil and process to a smooth paste.

2 Heat the remaining oil in a wok and add the paste. Cook for 3–4 minutes over low heat, stirring constantly until very fragrant. Add the curry powder and stir for another 2 minutes. Add the coconut milk, tamarind, kecap manis and 1 cup (250 ml/8 fl oz) water to the wok. Bring to the boil, stirring occasionally, then reduce the heat and simmer for 10 minutes.

3 Add the fish, tomato and lemon juice and season well. Simmer for 5 minutes or until the fish is just cooked. Serve immediately.

NUTRITION PER SERVE
Protein 22 g; Fat 30 g; Carbohydrate 6.5 g;
Dietary Fibre 4 g; Cholesterol 65 mg;
1600 kJ (382 Cal)

NOTE: Fish curry powder is a blend of spices suited to seafood flavours. It is available from Asian food stores.

Process the ingredients to make a smooth paste, then stir-fry over low heat for 3–4 minutes.

Add the coconut milk to the paste and simmer the sauce for 10 minutes, stirring occasionally.

Add the fish, tomato and lemon juice and season with salt and pepper.

LAMB KOFTA CURRY

Preparation time: 25 minutes
Total cooking time: 35 minutes
Serves 4

500 g (1 lb) minced lean lamb
1 onion, finely chopped
1 clove garlic, finely chopped
1 teaspoon grated fresh ginger
1 small fresh chilli, finely chopped
1 teaspoon garam masala
1 teaspoon ground coriander
1/4 cup (45 g/1 1/2 oz) ground almonds
2 tablespoons chopped fresh
    coriander leaves

SAUCE
2 teaspoons oil
1 onion, finely chopped
3 tablespoons Korma curry paste
400 g (13 oz) can chopped tomatoes
1/2 cup (125 g/4 oz) low-fat plain
    yoghurt
1 teaspoon lemon juice

1 Combine the lamb, onion, garlic, ginger, chilli, garam masala, ground coriander, ground almonds and 1 teaspoon salt in a large bowl. Shape the mixture into walnut-sized balls with your hands.

2 Heat a large non-stick frying pan and cook the koftas in batches until brown on both sides—they don't have to be cooked all the way through.

3 Meanwhile, to make the sauce, heat the oil in a large saucepan over low heat. Add the onion and cook for 6–8 minutes, or until soft and golden. Add the curry paste and cook until fragrant. Add the chopped tomatoes and simmer for 5 minutes. Stir in the yoghurt (1 tablespoon at a time) and the lemon juice until combined.

4 Place the koftas in the tomato sauce. Cook, covered, over low heat for 20 minutes. Serve over steamed rice and garnish with the chopped coriander.

NUTRITION PER SERVE
Protein 32 g; Fat 23 g; Carbohydrate 10 g;
Dietary Fibre 5 g; Cholesterol 88 mg;
1575 kJ (375 Cal)

Roll the lamb mixture into walnut-sized balls with your hands.

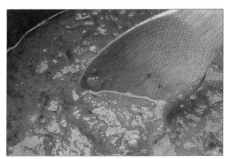

Add the chopped tomatoes and simmer for 5 minutes.

Add the koftas to the tomato sauce and cook over low heat for 20 minutes.

NONYA LIME CHICKEN

Preparation time: 20 minutes
Total cooking time: 25 minutes
Serves 4–6

2/3 cup (90 g/3 oz) Asian shallots
4 cloves garlic
2 stems lemon grass, white part only, chopped
2 teaspoons finely chopped fresh galangal
1 teaspoon ground turmeric
2 tablespoons sambal oelek
1 tablespoon shrimp paste
1/4 cup (60 ml/2 fl oz) oil

1 kg (2 lb) chicken thigh fillets, cut into cubes
410 ml (13 fl oz) coconut milk
1 teaspoon finely grated lime rind
1/2 cup (125 ml/4 fl oz) lime juice
6 kaffir lime leaves, finely shredded
2 tablespoons tamarind concentrate
lime wedges and kaffir lime leaves, to garnish

1 Place the shallots, garlic, lemon grass, galangal, turmeric, sambal oelek and shrimp paste in a blender and blend until smooth.
2 Heat a wok until very hot, add the oil and swirl to coat. Add the spice paste and stir-fry for 1–2 minutes, or until fragrant. Add the chicken and stir-fry for 5 minutes, or until browned.
3 Add the coconut milk, lime rind and juice, lime leaves and tamarind concentrate. Reduce the heat and simmer for 15 minutes, or until the chicken is cooked and the sauce has reduced and thickened slightly. Season well with salt. Garnish with lime wedges and lime leaves to serve.

NUTRITION PER SERVE (6)
Protein 32 g; Fat 25 g; Carbohydrate 4 g; Dietary Fibre 1.5 g; Cholesterol 65 mg; 1590 kJ (380 cal)

Fresh galangal is similar to fresh ginger. Peel it and then finely chop or grate.

Blend the shallots, garlic, lemon grass, galangal, turmeric, sambal oelek and shrimp paste.

Stir-fry the chicken in the spice paste for 5 minutes or until it is browned.

CRAB CURRY

Preparation time: 25 minutes
Total cooking time: 20 minutes
Serves 6

4 raw large blue swimmer or mud
   crabs
1 tablespoon oil
1 large onion, finely chopped
2 cloves garlic, crushed
1 stem lemon grass, white part only,
   finely chopped
1 teaspoon sambal oelek
1 teaspoon ground cumin
1 teaspoon ground turmeric
1 teaspoon ground coriander

270 ml (9 fl oz) light coconut cream
2 cups (500 ml/16 fl oz) chicken stock
$1/3$ cup (20 g/$3/4$ oz) firmly packed
   fresh basil leaves

1 Pull back the apron and remove the top shell from the crabs. Remove the intestines and grey feathery gills. Cut each crab into four pieces. Use a cracker to crack the claws open; this will make it easier to eat later and will also allow the flavours to get into the crab meat.
2 Heat the oil in a large saucepan or wok. Add the chopped onion, crushed garlic, lemon grass and sambal oelek, and cook for 2–3 minutes, or until softened but not brown.

3 Add the cumin, turmeric, coriander and $1/2$ teaspoon salt, and cook for a further 2 minutes, or until fragrant.
4 Stir in the coconut cream and stock. Bring to the boil, then reduce the heat, add the crab pieces and cook, stirring occasionally, for 10 minutes, or until the liquid has reduced and thickened slightly and the crabs are cooked through. Stir in the basil and serve with steamed rice.

NUTRITION PER SERVE
Protein 0.5 g; Fat 7 g; Carbohydrate 1.5 g;
Dietary Fibre 0.5 g; Cholesterol 20 mg;
290 kJ (70 Cal)

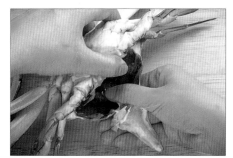

Pull back the apron and remove the top shell from the crab.

Remove the intestines and grey feathery gills from the crab.

Crack the claws open to allow the flavours to get into the crab meat while it is cooking.

CHICKEN AND PEANUT PANANG CURRY

Preparation time: 25 minutes
Total cooking time: 30–40 minutes
Serves 4

1 tablespoon oil
1 large red onion, chopped
1–2 tablespoons Panang curry paste
1 cup (250 ml/4 fl oz) coconut milk
500 g (1 lb) chicken thigh fillets, cut into bite-sized pieces
4 kaffir lime leaves
1/4 cup (60 g/2 oz) coconut cream
1 tablespoon fish sauce
1 tablespoon lime juice

2 teaspoons soft brown sugar
1/2 cup (80 g/2³/4 oz) roasted peanuts, chopped
1/2 cup (15 g/1/2 oz) Thai basil leaves
1/2 cup (80 g/2³/4 oz) chopped fresh pineapple
1 Lebanese cucumber, sliced
chilli sauce, to serve

1 Heat the oil in a wok or large frying pan. Add the onion and curry paste to the wok and stir over medium heat for 2 minutes. Add the coconut milk and bring to the boil.
2 Add the chicken and kaffir lime leaves to the wok, then reduce the heat and cook for 15 minutes. Remove the chicken with a wire mesh strainer or slotted spoon. Simmer the sauce for 5 minutes, or until it is reduced and quite thick.
3 Return the chicken to the wok. Add the coconut cream, fish sauce, lime juice and brown sugar. Cook for 5 minutes. Stir in the peanuts, basil and pineapple. Serve with the sliced cucumber on the side, some chilli sauce, as well as steamed rice.

NUTRITION PER SERVE
Protein 40 g; Fat 40 g; Carbohydrate 16 g; Dietary Fibre 5 g; Cholesterol 63 mg; 2466 kJ (590 cal)

Add the red onion and curry paste to the hot oil and stir with a wooden spoon.

Remove the cooked chicken from the wok and set it aside while cooking the sauce.

Stir in the chopped peanuts, basil and pineapple just before serving.

LAMB NECK CURRY

Preparation time: 30 minutes
Total cooking time: 1 hour 35 minutes
Serves 4–6

1 tablespoon oil
8 best lamb neck chops (see NOTE)
2 onions, sliced
3 cloves garlic, finely chopped
2 teaspoons finely chopped fresh
   ginger
1 small green chilli, seeded and finely
   chopped
1/2 teaspoon ground cumin
1 teaspoon ground fennel
1 1/2 teaspoons ground turmeric
1 1/2 teaspoons chilli powder
2 teaspoons garam masala
1 star anise
1 cinnamon stick
5 curry leaves
2 bay leaves
2 cups (500 ml/16 fl oz) beef stock
8 tomatoes, peeled and quartered

1 Heat the oil in a large frying pan, add the lamb and cook in batches for 5–8 minutes, or until browned. Place in a large saucepan.

2 Add the onion to the frying pan and cook, stirring frequently, for 5 minutes, or until soft and browned. Stir in the garlic, ginger and green chilli and cook for 1 minute. Then stir in the cumin, fennel, turmeric, chilli powder, garam masala, star anise, cinnamon stick, curry leaves and bay leaves, and cook, stirring to prevent sticking, for a further 1 minute.

3 Add 2 tablespoons cold water to the frying pan, mix well, and then add the beef stock. Bring to the boil, then pour over the lamb. Stir in the tomato, reduce the heat and simmer, covered, for 1 hour 15 minutes. Serve with jasmine rice tossed with coriander.

NUTRITION PER SERVE (6)
Protein 17 g; Fat 7 g; Carbohydrate 5 g; Dietary Fibre 5 g; Cholesterol 48 mg; 658 kJ (157 Cal)

NOTE: Best lamb neck chops come from the meat just under the shoulder and are sweeter, leaner and meatier than lamb neck.

Cook the lamb neck chops in batches until browned.

Stir the spices to prevent them sticking to the base of the pan.

SAAG GOSHT (LAMB AND SPINACH CURRY)

Preparation time: 30 minutes
Total cooking time: 2 hours 20 minutes
Serves 6

1 kg (2 lb) English spinach
1/2 cup (125 ml/4 fl oz) oil
1.5 kg (3 lb) lamb, cut into
    3 cm (1 1/4 inch) cubes (see NOTE)
2 red onions, finely chopped
6 cloves garlic, crushed
1 1/2 tablespoons grated fresh ginger
2 bay leaves
2 tablespoons ground coriander
1 tablespoon ground cumin
1 teaspoon ground turmeric
2 large vine-ripened tomatoes, peeled,
    seeded and chopped
2–3 small green chillies, seeded and
    finely chopped
100 g (3 1/2 oz) plain thick yoghurt
1 cinnamon stick
2 teaspoons garam masala

1 Preheat the oven to warm 170°C (325°F/Gas 3). Trim the spinach and quickly blanch in simmering water. Drain, cool slightly and squeeze to remove any excess moisture, then place in a food processor and process until smooth.
2 Heat half the oil in a large saucepan. Add the lamb pieces in batches and cook over high heat for 4–5 minutes, or until browned. Remove the lamb from the pan.
3 Heat the remaining oil in the saucepan. Add the onion and cook, stirring frequently, for 10 minutes, or until golden brown but not burnt. Add the garlic, ginger and bay leaves, and cook, stirring, for 3 more minutes.

4 Add the spices and cook, stirring, for 2 minutes, or until fragrant. Add the tomato and chilli, and stir over low heat for 5 minutes, or until the tomato is thick and pulpy. Remove from the heat and cool for 5 minutes. Transfer to a 4 litre ovenproof casserole dish and stir in the yoghurt.
5 Add the meat to the dish and add the cinnamon stick and 1 teaspoon salt. Bake, covered, for 1 hour and then uncovered for a further 15 minutes. Stir in the spinach and garam masala, and cook, stirring

occasionally, for 15 minutes, or until the meat is tender. Remove the bay leaves and cinnamon stick, and serve with rice or pilaf.

NUTRITION PER SERVE
Protein 60 g; Fat 30 g; Carbohydrate 5 g; Dietary Fibre 6.5 g; Cholesterol 170 mg; 2240 kJ (533 Cal)

NOTE: Ask your butcher to bone and cut a leg of lamb into 3 cm (1 1/4 inch) cubes. A 2.2 kg (4 lb 7 oz) leg will yield about 1.5 kg (3 lb) meat.

Squeeze the blanched spinach to remove any excess moisture.

Process the spinach in a food processor until smooth.

Stir over low heat until the tomato is thick and pulpy.

COUNTRY CHICKEN KAPITAN

Preparation time: 35 minutes
Total cooking time: 35 minutes
Serves 4–6

30 g (1 oz) small dried prawns
4 tablespoons oil
4–8 red chillies, seeded and finely
    chopped
4 cloves garlic, finely chopped
3 stems lemon grass (white part only),
    finely chopped
2 teaspoons turmeric
10 candlenuts
2 large onions, chopped
1/4 teaspoon salt
1 cup (250 ml/8 fl oz) coconut milk
500 g (1 lb) chicken thigh fillets,
    cut into bite-sized pieces
1/2 cup (125 ml/4 fl oz) coconut cream
2 tablespoons lime juice

1 Dry-fry the prawns over low heat for 3 minutes, shaking the wok regularly, until they are dark orange and have a strong aroma. Pound in a mortar and pestle until finely ground, or process in a small food processor.
2 Mix half the oil with the chilli, garlic, lemon grass, turmeric and candlenuts in a food processor, in short bursts, regularly scraping the bowl, until very finely chopped.
3 Add the remaining oil to a large wok and cook the onion and salt over low heat, stirring regularly, for 8 minutes, or until golden. Add the spice mixture and nearly all the ground prawns, setting a little aside to use as garnish. Stir for 5 minutes. If the mixture begins to stick to the bottom of the wok, add 2 tablespoons of the coconut milk. It is important for the

flavour to cook this thoroughly.
4 Add the chicken and stir well. Cook for 5 minutes or until the chicken begins to brown. Stir in the coconut milk and 1 cup (250 ml/8 fl oz) water and bring to the boil. Reduce the heat and simmer for 7 minutes or until the chicken is cooked and the sauce is thick. Add the coconut cream and

bring back to the boil, stirring constantly. Add the lime juice and serve immediately, sprinkled with the reserved ground prawns.

NUTRITION PER SERVE (6)
Protein 22 g; Fat 15 g; Carbohydrate 5.5 g;
Dietary Fibre 2.5 g; Cholesterol 50 mg;
1020 kJ (245 cal)

Pound the dry-fried prawns in a mortar and pestle until finely ground.

Process the chilli mixture in shorts bursts, regularly scraping the side of the bowl.

Stir-fry the onion and spice mixture for 5 minutes, taking care not to let it stick.

FISH HOTPOT WITH GINGER AND TOMATOES

Preparation time: 20 minutes +
  20 minutes soaking
Total cooking time: 1 hour
Serves 4

1 tablespoon peanut oil
1 onion, cut into thin wedges
1 small fresh red chilli, sliced
3 cloves garlic, finely chopped
2 cm x 2 cm (3/4 x 3/4 inch) piece
    fresh ginger, julienned
1/2 teaspoon ground turmeric
425 g (14 oz) can diced tomatoes
1 litre chicken stock
1 tablespoon tamarind purée
80 g (3 oz) dried flat rice stick
    noodles
600 g (11/4 lb) snapper fillets,
    skin removed, cut into 3 cm
    (11/4 inch) cubes
fresh coriander leaves, to garnish

1 Preheat the oven to hot 220°C
(425°F/Gas 7). Heat the oil in a large
frying pan over medium–high heat
and cook the onion wedges for
1–2 minutes, or until softened. Add
the chilli, chopped garlic and ginger
and cook for 30 seconds. Add the
ground turmeric, tomato, chicken
stock and tamarind purée and bring
to the boil over high heat. Transfer
to a 2.5 litre (80 fl oz) heatproof hotpot
or flameproof casserole dish and cook,
covered, in the oven for 40 minutes.
2 Place the noodles in a large
heatproof bowl, cover with warm
water and soak for 15–20 minutes,
or until *al dente*. Drain, rinse and
drain again.
3 Remove the hotpot from the oven
and stir in the noodles. Add the fish
cubes, then cover and return to the
oven for a further 10 minutes, or
until the fish is cooked through.
Serve sprinkled with some fresh
coriander leaves.

NUTRITION PER SERVE
Protein 36 g; Fat 8 g; Carbohydrate 23.5 g;
Dietary Fibre 3 g; Cholesterol 91.5 mg;
1310 kJ (315 Cal)

Gently add all the fish cubes to the hotpot
mixture.

BALTI-STYLE LAMB

Preparation time: 15 minutes
Total cooking time: 1 hour 25 minutes
Serves 4

1 kg (2 lb) lamb leg steaks, cut into
    3 cm (1¼ inch) cubes
1 tablespoon Balti masala paste
2 tablespoons ghee or oil
3 cloves garlic, crushed
1 tablespoon garam masala
1 large onion, finely chopped
4 tablespoons Balti masala paste,
    extra
2 tablespoons chopped fresh
    coriander leaves
fresh coriander leaves, extra,
    to garnish

1 Preheat the oven to moderately hot 190°C (375°F/Gas 5). Place the meat, masala paste and 1½ cups (375 ml/12 fl oz) boiling water in a 4 litre ovenproof casserole dish, and combine. Cook, covered, in the oven for 30–40 minutes, or until almost cooked through. Drain, reserving the stock.

2 Heat the ghee in a wok, add the garlic and garam masala, and stir-fry over medium heat for 1 minute. Add the onion and cook for 5–7 minutes, or until the onion is soft and golden brown. Increase the heat, add the extra masala paste and the lamb. Cook for 5 minutes to brown the meat. Slowly add the reserved stock and simmer over low heat, stirring occasionally, for 15 minutes.

3 Add the chopped coriander leaves and 1 cup (250 ml/8 fl oz) water and simmer for 15 minutes, or until the meat is tender and the sauce has thickened slightly. Season with salt and ground black pepper. Garnish with the extra coriander leaves and serve with roti or naan bread.

NUTRITION PER SERVE
Protein 58 g; Fat 8.5 g; Carbohydrate 3.5 g;
Dietary Fibre 1 g; Cholesterol 167 mg;
1368 kJ (327 Cal)

Cook the meat until almost cooked through, then drain, reserving the liquid.

Cook the onion over medium heat until soft and golden brown.

Simmer until the meat is tender and the sauce has thickened slightly.

141

MUSAMAN (THAI BEEF CURRY WITH POTATO AND PEANUTS)

Preparation time: 30 minutes
Total cooking time: 1 hour 45 minutes
Serves 4

1 tablespoon tamarind pulp
2 tablespoons oil
750 g (1½ lb) lean stewing beef,
    cubed
2 cups (500 ml/16 fl oz) coconut milk
4 cardamom pods, bruised
2 cups (500 ml/16 fl oz) coconut
    cream
2–3 tablespoons Musaman curry
    paste
8 pickling onions, peeled
    (see NOTE)
8 baby potatoes, peeled
    (see NOTE)
2 tablespoons fish sauce
2 tablespoons palm sugar
½ cup (70 g/2¼ oz) unsalted
    peanuts, roasted and ground
fresh coriander leaves,
    to garnish

1 Combine the tamarind pulp and ½ cup (125 ml/4 fl oz) boiling water and leave to cool. Mash the pulp until dissolved, then strain and reserve the liquid. Discard the pulp.
2 Heat the oil in a wok or a large saucepan and cook the beef in batches over high heat for 5 minutes, or until browned. Reduce the heat and add the coconut milk and cardamom to the pan, and simmer for 1 hour, or until the beef is tender. Remove the beef, strain and reserve the beef and cooking liquid.
3 Heat the coconut cream in the wok and stir in the curry paste. Cook for

5 minutes, or until the oil starts to separate from the cream.
4 Add the onions, potatoes, fish sauce, palm sugar, peanuts, beef mixture, reserved liquid and tamarind water, and simmer for 25–30 minutes. Garnish with fresh coriander leaves. Serve with rice.

NUTRITION PER SERVE
Protein 52 g; Fat 77 g; Carbohydrate 35 g;
Dietary Fibre 7.5 g; Cholesterol 115 mg;
4324 kJ (1033 Cal)

NOTE: Use small onions and potatoes, about 25–30 g (¾ oz–1 oz) each.

Mash the tamarind pulp with a fork, then strain and reserve the liquid.

Cook the beef in batches over high heat until browned.

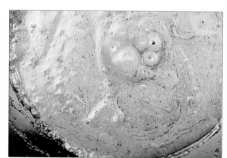

Cook until the oil starts to separate from the cream.

WHITE-COOKED CHICKEN WITH SPRING ONION SAUCE

Preparation time: 5 minutes
Total cooking time: 1 hour
  + 1 hour chilling
Serves 6

1.8 kg (3 lb 10 oz) chicken
3 slices fresh ginger
1¹/₂ teaspoons salt
iced water (see Hint)

SPRING ONION SAUCE
2 tablespoons oil
3 spring onions, thinly sliced
1 tablespoon soy sauce

1 Remove any pockets of fat from the chicken, then remove and discard the tail. Place the chicken in a large pan and add enough water to cover. Add the ginger and salt and bring to the boil. Cover and simmer for 20 minutes.
2 Turn off the heat, keeping the pan covered tightly. Set aside for 35 minutes. Remove the chicken carefully from the pan, draining off any of the stock that has lodged inside. Plunge the chicken into a large bowl of iced water. This process stops the chicken cooking and tightens the skin, sealing in the juices.
3 Leave the cooled chicken in the bowl of iced water and chill in the refrigerator for 1 hour. Just before serving, drain the chicken from the water and chop, Chinese-style.
4 To make the spring onion sauce, heat the oil in a wok, add the spring onion and cook briefly just to heat through. Stir in the soy sauce. Serve the chicken with the spring onion sauce poured over.

NUTRITION PER SERVE
Protein 50 g; Fat 11 g; Carbohydrate 0.5 g; Dietary Fibre 0 g; Cholesterol 110 mg; 1265 kJ (302 cal)

HINT: Use this recipe whenever cold, boiled chicken is called for. Because the chicken never boils and is chilled very rapidly, the juices are sealed in and the result is very succulent, moist and tender. To achieve the result required, it is essential that the water into which the chicken is plunged is very well chilled. Add 2 or 3 trays of ice cubes to ensure that it is as cold as possible.

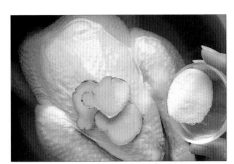

Cover the chicken with water and add the ginger slices and salt.

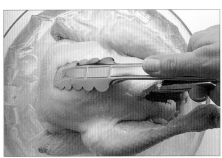

Plunge the chicken into a large bowl filled with iced water to stop the cooking process.

Just before serving, drain the chicken from the water and chop Chinese-style.

BURMESE PORK CURRY

Preparation time: 30 minutes
Total cooking time: 1 hour
Serves 6

2 stems lemon grass, white part only, sliced
1 red onion, chopped
1 clove garlic
1 teaspoon grated fresh ginger
2 large red dried chillies
1 teaspoon fenugreek seeds, roasted and ground
1 teaspoon yellow mustard seeds, roasted and ground
2 teaspoons paprika
2 tablespoons Worcestershire sauce

750 g (1 1/2 lb) lean boneless shoulder pork, cut into cubes
2 tablespoons fish sauce
6 chat potatoes, peeled and sliced
2 small red onions, diced
1 tablespoon oil
2 tablespoons mango chutney

1 Put the lemon grass, onion, garlic, ginger, chillies, fenugreek seeds, yellow mustard seeds, paprika and Worcestershire sauce in a processor or blender and mix to a thick paste.
2 Place the pork in a bowl, sprinkle with the fish sauce and 1/4 teaspoon ground black pepper and toss to coat.
3 Place the potato and onion in another bowl, add 3 tablespoons of the paste and toss to coat. Add the

remaining paste to the pork. Mix well.
4 Heat the oil in a wok over medium heat. Add the pork cubes and cook in batches, stirring, for 8 minutes, or until the meat begins to brown. Remove from the pan. Add the potato and onion and cook, stirring, for 5 minutes, or until soft and starting to brown.
5 Return the meat to the pan and stir in 3 cups (750 ml/24 fl oz) water, adding 1 cup (250 ml/8 fl oz) at a time. Stir in the mango chutney, then reduce the heat and simmer for 30 minutes, or until the meat and potatoes are tender.

NUTRITION PER SERVE
Protein 30 g; Fat 8.5 g; Carbohydrate 16 g; Dietary Fibre 2.5 g; Cholesterol 60 mg; 1126 kJ (270 Cal)

Process all the spice paste ingredients to make a thick paste.

Heat the oil in a saucepan or wok and brown the pork in batches.

Add the potato and onion and cook until they are starting to brown.

CHICKEN DUMPLINGS IN GREEN CURRY

Preparation time: 25 minutes
  + 2–3 hours refrigeration
Total cooking time: 35 minutes
Serves 3–4

500 g (1 lb) chicken mince
3 spring onions, finely chopped
2 tablespoons small fresh coriander
  leaves
1 stem lemon grass, white part only,
  thinly sliced
1/4 cup (60 ml/2 fl oz) fish sauce
1 teaspoon chicken stock powder
1 1/2 cups (280 g/9 oz) cooked jasmine
  rice

1 egg, plus 1 egg white
2 teaspoons oil
2 tablespoons green curry paste
2 x 400 ml (13 fl oz) cans coconut milk
4 fresh kaffir lime leaves
1/2 cup (15 g/1/2 oz) fresh basil leaves
1 tablespoon lemon juice

1 Mix together the chicken mince, spring onion, coriander leaves, lemon grass, 2 tablespoons of the fish sauce, stock powder and some pepper. Add the rice and mix well with your hands.
2 In a separate bowl, beat the egg and egg white with electric beaters until thick and creamy and then fold into the chicken mixture. With lightly floured hands, roll tablespoons of the mixture into balls. Place on a tray,

cover and refrigerate for 2–3 hours, or until firm.
3 Heat the oil in a large frying pan, add the green curry paste and stir over medium heat for 1 minute. Gradually stir in the coconut milk, then reduce the heat to simmer. Add the lime leaves and chicken dumplings to the sauce; cover and simmer for 25–30 minutes, stirring occasionally. Stir in the basil leaves, remaining fish sauce and lemon juice. Serve with steamed rice.

NUTRITION PER SERVE (4)
Protein 37 g; Fat 46 g; Carbohydrate 30 g; Dietary Fibre 4.5 g; Cholesterol 110 mg; 2815 kJ (672 cal)

Beat the egg and egg white with electric beaters until thick and creamy.

Flour your hands and roll tablespoons of the mixture into balls.

When the sauce is simmering, add the lime leaves and chicken dumplings.

FISH KOFTAS IN TOMATO CURRY SAUCE

Preparation time: 40 minutes
Total cooking time: 30 minutes
Serves 6

750 g (1½ lb) firm fish fillets, such as snapper or ling, roughly chopped
1 onion, chopped
2–3 cloves garlic, chopped
1 tablespoon grated fresh ginger
4 tablespoons chopped fresh coriander leaves
1 teaspoon garam masala
¼ teaspoon chilli powder
1 egg, lightly beaten
oil, for shallow-frying

TOMATO CURRY SAUCE
2 tablespoons oil
1 large onion, finely chopped
3–4 cloves garlic, finely chopped
1 tablespoon grated fresh ginger
1 teaspoon ground turmeric
1 teaspoon ground cumin
1 teaspoon ground coriander
½ teaspoon garam masala
¼ teaspoon chilli powder
2 x 400 g (13 oz) cans crushed tomatoes
3 tablespoons chopped fresh coriander

1 Place the fish in a food processor and process until smooth. Add the onion, garlic, ginger, coriander leaves, garam masala, chilli powder and egg, and process using the pulse button, until well combined. Using wetted hands, form 1 tablespoon of the mixture into a ball. Repeat with the remaining mixture.
2 To make the tomato curry sauce, heat the oil in a large saucepan, add the onion, garlic and ginger, and cook, stirring frequently, over medium heat for 8 minutes, or until lightly golden.
3 Add the spices and cook, stirring, for 2 minutes, or until aromatic. Add the tomato and 1 cup (250 ml/8 fl oz) water, then reduce the heat and simmer, stirring frequently, for 15 minutes, or until reduced and thickened.

4 Meanwhile, heat the oil in a large frying pan to the depth of 2 cm (¾ inch). Add the fish koftas in 3–4 batches and cook for 3 minutes, or until browned all over. Drain on paper towels.
5 Add the koftas to the sauce and simmer over low heat for 5 minutes, or until heated through. Gently fold in the coriander, season with salt to taste and serve with steamed rice and freshly made chapatis.

NUTRITION PER SERVE
Protein 30 g; Fat 15 g; Carbohydrate 7 g; Dietary Fibre 3 g; Cholesterol 118 mg; 1145 kJ (273 Cal)

NOTE: The fish mixture is quite moist. Wetting your hands will stop the mixture from sticking to them.

Using wetted hands, form tablespoons of the mixture into balls.

Cook the onion, garlic and ginger until lightly golden.

INDONESIAN CHICKEN IN COCONUT MILK

Preparation time: 15 minutes
+ 1 hour marinating time
Total cooking time: 50 minutes
Serves 4

8 large or 12 small chicken
   drumsticks
2 teaspoons crushed garlic
1 teaspoon salt
1/2 teaspoon ground black
   pepper
2 teaspoons ground cumin
2 teaspoons ground coriander
1/2 teaspoon ground fennel
1/2 teaspoon ground
   cinnamon
1/4 cup (60 ml/2 fl oz) oil
2 onions, thinly sliced
3/4 cup (185 ml/6 fl oz)
   coconut milk
1 tablespoon lemon juice or
   malt vinegar

1 Pat the chicken drumsticks dry with paper towels. Place the chicken in a large glass or ceramic bowl. Combine the garlic, salt, pepper, cumin, coriander, fennel, cinnamon and 2 tablespoons of the oil. Rub the mixture thoroughly over the chicken. Cover and marinate for 1 hour in the refrigerator.
2 Heat the remaining oil in a large pan. Add the onion and cook, stirring, until it is soft and golden. Add the chicken drumsticks and cook quickly over medium-high heat until they are well browned.
3 Combine the coconut milk, 1 cup (250 ml/8 fl oz) water and the lemon juice. Pour over the chicken, cover and simmer until the chicken is tender and the sauce is well reduced. (This should take about 40 minutes.) Serve the chicken with rice.

NUTRITION PER SERVE
Protein 44 g; Fat 28 g; Carbohydrate 4.5 g;
Dietary Fibre 2 g; Cholesterol 95 mg;
1870 kJ (445 cal)

Rub the garlic and spice mixture thoroughly over the chicken drumsticks.

Add the marinated chicken to the onion and cook over medium-high heat until well browned.

Combine the coconut milk, water and lemon juice, and pour over the chicken.

GREEN FISH CURRY

Preparation time: 15 minutes
Total cooking time: 15 minutes
Serves 4

1 tablespoon peanut oil
1 brown onion, chopped
1¹/₂ tablespoons green curry paste
1¹/₂ cups (375 ml/12 fl oz) coconut
   milk
700 g (1 lb 6¹/₂ oz) boneless firm white
   fish fillets, cut in bite-sized pieces

3 kaffir lime leaves
1 tablespoon fish sauce
2 teaspoons grated palm sugar
2 tablespoons lime juice
1 long green chilli, finely sliced

1 Heat a wok until very hot, add the oil and swirl to coat. Add the onion and stir-fry for 2 minutes, or until soft. Add the curry paste and stir-fry for 1–2 minutes, or until fragrant. Stir in the coconut milk and bring to the boil.
2 Add the fish and lime leaves to the wok, reduce the heat and simmer, stirring occasionally, for 8–10 minutes, or until the fish is cooked through.
3 Stir in the fish sauce, palm sugar and lime juice. Scatter the chilli slices over the curry before serving with steamed rice.

NUTRITION PER SERVE
Protein 39 g; Fat 29 g; Carbohydrate 4.5 g;
Dietary Fibre 1 g; Cholesterol 123.5 mg;
1820 kJ (435 Cal)

SUGGESTED FISH: Ling, ocean perch, bream, warehou.

To prevent skin irritation, wear rubber gloves when slicing the chilli.

Heat the coconut milk to boiling point before adding the fish.

Gently simmer the fish pieces, stirring occasionally, until cooked through.

RED VEGETABLE CURRY

Preparation time: 25 minutes
Total cooking time: 30 minutes
Serves 4

1 tablespoon oil
1 onion, chopped
1–2 tablespoons red curry paste
1 1/2 cups (375 ml/12 fl oz) coconut
    milk
2 potatoes, peeled and chopped
200 g (6 1/2 oz) cauliflower florets
6 kaffir lime leaves
150 g (5 oz) snake beans, cut into
    short lengths

1/2 red capsicum, cut into strips
10 fresh baby corn spears, cut in half
    lengthways (see NOTE)
1 tablespoon green peppercorns,
    roughly chopped
1/4 cup (7 g/1/4 oz) Thai basil leaves,
    finely chopped
2 tablespoons fish sauce
1 tablespoon lime juice
2 teaspoons soft brown sugar

1 Heat the oil in a large wok and stir-fry the onion and curry paste for
4 minutes over medium heat.
2 Add the coconut milk and 1 cup
(250 ml/8 fl oz) water, bring to the boil and simmer for 5 minutes. Add the

potatoes, cauliflower and kaffir lime leaves and simmer for 7 minutes. Add the snake beans, capsicum, corn and peppercorns and cook for 5 minutes or until the vegetables are tender.
3 Add the basil, fish sauce, lime juice and sugar just before serving.

NUTRITION PER SERVE
Protein 7.5 g; Fat 24 g; Carbohydrate 23 g;
Dietary Fibre 6 g; Cholesterol 0 mg;
1414 kJ (338 cal)

NOTE: You could use canned corn spears—add just before serving.

Stir the chopped onion and curry paste in a wok for 4 minutes over medium heat.

Add the snake beans, capsicum, corn and peppercorns and cook until tender.

When the vegetables are tender, add the basil, fish sauce, lime juice and sugar.

Curry Accompaniments

CUCUMBER RAITA

Peel and finely chop 2 Lebanese cucumbers and combine with 1 cup (250 g/8 oz) plain yoghurt in a small bowl. Set aside. Fry 1 teaspoon each of ground cumin and mustard seeds in a dry pan for 1 minute, or until fragrant. Add the toasted spices to the yoghurt mixture with 1/2 teaspoon grated fresh ginger and mix well to combine. Season well with salt and black pepper and garnish with a pinch of paprika. Serve chilled. Makes about 2 cups.

COCONUT BANANAS

Peel 2 large bananas and cut into thick slices. Dip the slices into 1/3 cup (80 ml/2³/4 fl oz) lemon juice, then toss in enough desiccated coconut to coat each piece. Serve at room temperature. Makes about 2 cups.

NAAN BREAD

Sift 500 g (1 lb) plain flour, 1 teaspoon baking powder, 1/2 teaspoon bicarbonate of soda and 1 teaspoon salt into a large bowl. Add 1 beaten egg, 1 tablespoon melted ghee or butter, 1/2 cup (125 g/4 oz) natural yoghurt and gradually mix in approximately 1 cup (250 ml/8 fl oz) milk to form a soft dough. Leave in a warm place, covered with a damp cloth, for 2 hours. Preheat the oven to moderately hot 200°C (400°F/Gas 6). Turn onto a well-floured surface and knead for 2–3 minutes, until smooth. Divide the dough into 8 portions and roll each into an oval 15 cm (6 inches) long. Brush with water and place wet-side down onto greased baking trays. Brush the top of each naan with melted ghee or butter (you will need 2–3 tablespoons). Bake for 8–10 minutes, or until golden brown. Serve immediately. Makes 8.

SWEET MANGO CHUTNEY

Peel 3 large, green mangoes, remove the stones and chop the flesh into large slices. Sprinkle with salt. Remove the seeds from 2 red chillies and finely chop. Blend 1/2 teaspoon garam masala with 1 1/2 cups (330 g/11 oz) raw sugar and place in a large pan with 1 cup (250 ml/8 floz) white vinegar. Bring to the boil, then reduce the heat and simmer for 5 minutes. Add the mangoes, chillies, a finely grated 5 cm (2 inch) piece fresh ginger and 1/2 cup (95 g/3 oz) finely chopped dates. Simmer for 1 hour, or until the mango is tender. Pour into warm sterilized jars and seal. The chutney can be stored in the refrigerator for up to 1 month. Makes about 3 cups.

STEAMED FRAGRANT RICE

Wash 2 1/2 cups (500 g/1 lb) long-grain rice in a sieve until the water runs clear. In a large saucepan, fry 1–2 crushed cloves garlic and 2 tablespoons finely grated fresh ginger in 2 tablespoons oil, ghee or butter. Add 3 cups (750 ml/24 fl oz) water, bring to the boil and cook for 1 minute. Cover with a tight-fitting lid, reduce the heat to as low as possible and cook for 10–15 minutes, or until steam tunnels form on the surface and the rice is soft and swollen. Turn off the heat and leave the pan, covered, for 10 minutes. Fluff the rice with a fork. Serves 6–8.

LIME PICKLE

Cut 12 limes into 8 thin wedges, sprinkle with salt and set aside. In a dry pan, fry 2 teaspoons each of turmeric, cumin seeds, fennel seeds, fenugreek seeds, and 3 teaspoons brown or yellow mustard seeds for 1–2 minutes. Remove from the heat and grind to a fine powder in a mortar and pestle. Over low heat, fry 5 chopped green chillies, 4 sliced cloves of garlic and a grated 2.5 cm (1 inch) piece fresh ginger in 1 tablespoon oil until golden brown. Add 2 cups (500 ml/16 fl oz) oil, 1 tablespoon sugar, the lime wedges and spices. Simmer over low heat for 10 minutes, stirring occasionally. Spoon the pickle into warm sterilized jars and seal. Store in the refrigerator. Makes 4–5 cups.

TOMATO AND ONION RELISH

In a medium bowl, combine 2 large, chopped tomatoes, 2 tablespoons chopped fresh coriander, 2 small, thinly sliced red onions, 2 tablespoons lime juice and 1 teaspoon soft brown sugar. Season with salt and black pepper. Mix well. Cover with plastic wrap and refrigerate for 15 minutes before serving. Makes about 2 cups.

From left to right: Cucumber raita; Coconut bananas; Tomato and onion relish; Lime pickle; Sweet mango chutney; Naan bread; Steamed fragrant rice.

Sauces

As the majority of stir-fry recipes have Asian flavourings, many of them are enhanced by a chilli or dipping sauce for serving. You can also use the chilli sauces below as an ingredient when required in the recipe.

COOKED HOT CHILLI SAUCE

Chop 2 cloves of garlic and combine in a dry frying pan with 2 stems of finely chopped lemon grass, 6 chopped French shallots, 2–4 tablespoons of chopped, fresh red chillies and 2 chopped coriander roots. Stir for 5 minutes over low heat and then allow to cool. Place in a food processor with 2 teaspoons shrimp paste and 2 tablespoons soft brown sugar. Process for 20 seconds at a time, scraping down the side of the bowl each time, until the mixture forms a smooth paste. Add 2 tablespoons of fish sauce and 3 tablespoons of cold water and process until smooth. A little more water can be added if a thinner consistency is required. Refrigerate in an airtight container for up to 1 month.

QUICK CHILLI SAUCE

Trim the stems from 6 large, fresh red chillies. Cut the chillies open (remove the seeds for a milder flavour) and soak for 15 minutes in hot water. Place in a food processor with 3 tablespoons white vinegar, $1/3$ cup (90 g/3 oz) caster sugar, 1 teaspoon of salt and 4 chopped cloves of garlic. Process until smooth. Transfer to a small pan and cook for 15 minutes over medium heat, stirring frequently until the sauce has thickened. Allow to cool and then stir in 2 teaspoons fish sauce. Note: To make sweet chilli sauce, increase the sugar to 1 cup (250 g/8 oz).

Clockwise, from top right: Green Mango Hot Sauce; Tamarind and Chilli Dipping Sauce; Sour Dipping Sauce; Basic Dipping Sauce (Nam Prik); Quick Chilli Sauce; Cooked Hot Chilli Sauce

BASIC DIPPING SAUCE (NAM PRIK)

In a bowl, combine 3 tablespoons fish sauce, 1 tablespoon of white vinegar, 2–3 teaspoons of finely chopped fresh red chillies, 1 teaspoon of sugar and 2 teaspoons of chopped fresh coriander stems and stir until the sugar dissolves.

HOT GREEN MANGO SAUCE

Combine 2 chopped cloves of garlic, 3 chopped French shallots, 1/4 teaspoon of freshly ground black pepper, 1 teaspoon of dried shrimp and 1 teaspoon of shrimp paste in a mortar and pestle or small-bowled food processor. Pound or process until finely chopped and then stir in 1 tablespoon of soft brown sugar, 1/2 finely grated green mango and 2 tablespoons of cold water. This sauce is best used within 12 hours.

SOUR DIPPING SAUCE

In a bowl, combine 3 tablespoons of fish sauce, 2 tablespoons of white vinegar and 2 tablespoons of lime juice. Chopped fresh coriander leaves can be added if you are serving a Thai dish.

TAMARIND AND CHILLI DIPPING SAUCE

Heat 1 tablespoon of oil in a wok; add 4 finely chopped French shallots and 2 chopped cloves of garlic and stir for 2 minutes over low heat. Add 1–2 teaspoons of chopped fresh red chillies and stir-fry for 30 seconds. Add 3 tablespoons of tamarind purée and 1 tablespoon of soft brown sugar. Bring to the boil, stirring, and then reduce the heat and simmer for 5 minutes. Allow to cool before serving. Can be seasoned with a little lime juice.

Index

Published by Murdoch Books®, a division of Murdoch Magazines Pty Ltd.

Murdoch Books® Australia
Pier 8/9, 23 Hickson Road
Millers Point NSW 2000
Phone: (612) 4352 7000
Fax: (612) 4352 7026

Murdoch Books UK Limited
Erico House
6th Floor North
93–99 Upper Richmond Road
Putney, London SW15 2TG
Phone: + 44 (0) 8785 5995
Fax: + 44 (0) 8785 5985

Editorial Director: Diana Hill
Project Manager: Zoë Harpham
Editor: Stephanie Kistner
Creative Director: Marylouise Brammer
Designer: Annette Fitzgerald
Production: Monika Paratore
Recipes developed by the Murdoch Books Test Kitchen.

Chief Executive: Juliet Rogers
Publisher: Kay Scarlett

The Publisher gratefully acknowledges the contribution of the recipe writers, chefs,
photographers and stylists who worked on the material appearing in this publication.

National Library of Australia Cataloguing-in-Publication Data
Everyday Asian. Includes index. ISBN 1 74045 233 X.
1. Cookery, Asian. (Series: Everyday series (Sydney, NSW)).
641.595.

PRINTED IN CHINA by Toppan Printing Co. (HK) Ltd.
Printed 2004.

IMPORTANT: Those who might be at risk from the effects of salmonella food poisoning
(the elderly, pregnant women, young children and those suffering from immune deficiency diseases)
should consult their doctor with any concerns about eating raw eggs.

bicarbonate of soda	— baking soda	cream	— single cream	sambal oelek	— chilli paste
besan flour	— chickpea flour	flat-leaf parsley	— Italian parsley	snow pea	— mange tout
capsicum	— bell pepper	minced meat	— ground meat	spring onion	— scallion/shallot/green onion
cornflour	— cornstarch	plain flour	— all-purpose flour	thick cream	— double/heavy cream
		prawn	— shrimp	tomato paste (US)	— tomato purée (UK)